Praise for *The Sorrow Stone*

'Taken from the Icelandic sagas, this is an astounding retelling of the Gísli and *Eyrbyggja* story. [Gíslason] brings medieval Iceland to vivid life, as he reimagines the fate of a woman caught up in one of Iceland's most famous sagas.' *The Australian*

'Gíslason's prose is wonderfully controlled; it can be as stark and harsh as some of the landscapes he so beautifully describes, and at other times is imbued with a quiet but deeply felt lyricism ... Gíslason unlocks and opens the doors to Disa's story, and it might just blow you away.' *The Saturday Paper*

'Subtle, well paced and compelling ... Gíslason's expansive knowledge of Icelandic history and culture lends authenticity to his characters' actions and musings.' *Australian Book Review*

'Gíslason has created an observant, courageous and determined woman ... [and] a sense of place that is wholly believable and intriguing to read ... There is no other book like this.' *ArtsHub*

'Gripping ... A marvellous feat of character and storytelling.' *The AU Review*

'I was wholly and immediately immersed ... Like the epic Icelandic sagas that inspired this sparse, gritty, captivating novel, I have no doubt *The Sorrow Stone* will be read by generations to come.' *Readings Monthly*

Praise for *The Ash Burner*

'This is a beautifully written novel about the intensities of youth and of mourning, and the strangeness and potential tragedy of young love. Its characters are vivid, its landscapes evocative, and its narrative given shape and power by the revelation at the end.' ***The Sydney Morning Herald***

'Gíslason's prose is in itself a constant source of pleasure: wry, expressive and poised.' ***The Weekend Australian***

'At once contemplative and precise, *The Ash Burner* is an exquisitely written novel that left me deeply moved by its tender exploration of beauty and grief.' **Hannah Kent**

Praise for *The Promise of Iceland*

'A deeply charming account of displacement, of not really knowing where you come from and how that makes it difficult to know where you belong.' ***The Sunday Mail***

'[A] memorable, finely crafted book.' ***The Age***

'What Gíslason does particularly well is make a case for the significance of place in people's lives ... [Iceland is] beautifully realised in the book's pages.' ***The Canberra Times***

'A powerful memoir about landscape and identity.' ***The Advertiser***

Kári Gíslason is a writer and academic who teaches creative writing and literary studies at QUT. He is the author of *The Promise of Iceland* (UQP, 2011), which told the story of return journeys he's made to his birthplace, and the novels *The Ash Burner* (UQP, 2015) and *The Sorrow Stone* (UQP, 2022). He is also the co-author, with Richard Fidler, of *Saga Land* (HarperCollins, 2017), and has written works of travel journalism, essays, reviews and radio scripts.

RUNNING WITH PIRATES

On freedom, adventure, and fathers and sons

KÁRI GÍSLASON

First published 2024 by University of Queensland Press
PO Box 6042, St Lucia, Queensland 4067 Australia

The University of Queensland Press (UQP) acknowledges the Traditional Owners and their custodianship of the lands on which UQP operates. We pay our respects to their Ancestors and their descendants, who continue cultural and spiritual connections to Country. We recognise their valuable contributions to Australian and global society.

uqp.com.au
reception@uqp.com.au

Cover design by Lisa White
Typeset in Perpetua 13/17 pt by Post Pre-press Group, Brisbane
Boat illustration by the author
Author photograph by Nicholas Martin
Printed in Australia by McPherson's Printing Group

Australian Government

Creative
Australia

University of Queensland Press is assisted by the Australian Government through Creative Australia, its principal arts investment and advisory body.

A catalogue record for this book is available from the National Library of Australia

ISBN 978 0 7022 6870 0 (pbk)
ISBN 978 0 7022 7006 2 (epdf)
ISBN 978 0 7022 7007 9 (epub)

University of Queensland Press uses papers that are natural, renewable and recyclable products made from wood grown in well-managed forests and other controlled sources. The logging and manufacturing processes conform to the environmental regulations of the country of origin.

MIX
Paper | Supporting
responsible forestry
FSC
www.fsc.org   FSC® C001695

For
Finnur Kári and Magnús Oliver

Contents

1

Stranding

Corfu, September 1990

There comes a moment when one's first steps into adulthood slip out of view, and our young self becomes so distant that we begin to lose sight of them altogether. But it is possible, I think, to look for that person now and then: to remember who they were and who we might still be, deep down.

Find and hear them again, before it's too late.

I had recently turned eighteen, and, at the moment I would like to begin this story, I was sleeping on the floor next to hot air vents at the back of a grand old ferry that connected Brindisi in the heel of Italy with Athens. It was just before light, and my body ached from the steel panels I'd been lying on. I stood up and stretched and leant on the handrail, still cold and damp to the touch. Small waves tailed from the hull. The ship was slowing, falling quieter, as though to bend an ear to the morning stillness.

I wasn't alone. Paul, my often-jolly, sometimes-sarcastic travel mate, was walking down the side of the ferry, looking for me. We'd been good friends to begin with, having met each other four months earlier in Scotland, but it wasn't going so well now.

1

Our friendship was revealing its cracks, much like the paint on the ferry's cabin walls. During the crossing from Italy, we'd given up on getting any sleep on the deck, where we were meant to be. It was warm when the ferry left the docks, but once we'd cleared the coast and were on open sea, everyone around us pulled out sleeping bags and blankets. We weren't as prepared and had to search out pockets of warmth elsewhere. Mine was next to the hot air vents. The smell of engine air wasn't nice, but at least it was warm. Paul, meanwhile, disappeared inside: he'd said he was cold and miserable enough to risk a ticket inspector's wrath.

He had his pack across his shoulder and was waving cheerily. 'Did you sleep?' he asked as he reached me.

'Yes, quite a bit, in the end,' I said. 'Better than I expected. You?'

'Aye, not too shabby.'

A coastline was coming into view, not yet more distinct than white smoke – an outline of high mountains and valleys that seemed to slip into the sea like sand. 'That must be Albania,' I said. 'I can just make out Corfu, too.' We were approaching the famous island from the north, in a channel between the mainland and the first wooded headlands of the coast.

Paul rubbed his eyes. 'Have you ever seen anything like this?'

The light made a silken, fabric-like veil across the hills. Dawn seemed to refuse its stage call.

'Where are the ciggies, by the way?' he asked.

'I think someone nicked them.'

'Bastard,' he said, looking me in the eyes, even if he was referring to the thief. 'Who was it? I'll get him.'

'I don't know. I was asleep. I left the carton on the top of my bag. It's my fault.' A few nights before, in Rome, we'd seen a young woman getting mugged. A group of boys with newspapers surrounded her, waving the papers in her face while they snatched her handbag away. We'd run to help her, but it was all over in a flash. When we asked if we could do anything for her, she said, 'No, no,' and walked on. The theft had stayed with me, but truth be told I couldn't be sure that the cigarettes had been stolen. 'Maybe they slid off into the sea,' I said. 'I shouldn't be so certain.'

Paul turned to face the coastline. 'Never mind,' he said. Then, after a moment: 'Could you kindly update me on the money situation?'

I was in charge of the budget: it had been three weeks of trying to make five hundred pounds stretch across the Continent. 'You want to buy some more?' I asked.

'Aye, if Your Grace will allow it.'

'Simple,' I said. I took a crumpled five-hundred-lira note from my pocket.

'That's it?' he asked. 'What's that in royal sterling, then?'

'About twenty pence,' I said.

Paul sighed. 'So, it's over, then? Bye-bye, freedom. Bye-bye, you pair of stupid, wandering sods. Back to reality you go.'

The realities that awaited each of us back home were rather different. I won't go into those details yet. The important thing at this moment, as the ferry slowed yet more, perhaps waiting for permission to enter the final stretch, is that neither Paul nor I could accept that our travels were over, because there was still too much to sort out in our heads. We were struggling with things that could only be sorted out from a distance, such as on an island where we'd never been before.

The tip of the sun made it over the horizon and dark orange struck the island. A town appeared, at first chalky and pale, then firelit, the buildings crowding the shore, queuing to get to a seafront esplanade and the walls of the port. Corfu Town. Other passengers began to prepare to disembark. We could, too, if we wanted. Our tickets allowed a stopover on the way to Athens.

'How about one more go,' Paul suggested. 'There could be work here.' He started the planning out loud; he seldom kept his thought processes to himself. 'Where would we sleep tonight? I mean, if we get off. What do we eat, eh?' He laughed at the absurdity of the question. 'What can you get in Corfu for twenty pence?'

'A packet of mints,' I said.

We smiled at each other with an awareness of how exposed and dumb we were – and had been the whole way across Europe. Now, no money at all. If we got off the ferry, there was nowhere to stay. We'd have to sleep outside on park benches or at the ferry terminal until we found a job. I couldn't even keep hold of a carton of cigarettes. What would happen to us if we had to sleep out in the open for a few nights? The best thing was to stay on the ferry all the way to Athens and scramble a way home. Call our mums. Accept failure. Take safety.

Paul read my thoughts. 'No-one's gonna murder us,' he said. 'We're not worth the trouble. Not me, anyway.'

'I'd give it a go,' I said.

'Aye, you would.'

Paul smiled again and I felt a faint pulse of what had drawn us together when we first met. A sympathy, an understanding. Nothing was as light as it was then; for each of us, there was too much riding on this trip. Too much weight. But dawn found some of our old levity, and without another word we picked up our packs. We would be runaways for a bit longer.

I loved first arrivals with all my heart and still do. The slight chaos of gates and platforms, the dislocation of all things being at once familiar and different. The hazy illusion of your own newness that you get by being somewhere new.

That morning, the docks of Corfu Town were very merry, and my mood stayed high with all the activity around us. Hostel workers and vans crowded the gangplanks. In every direction, special offers were being proclaimed alongside promises of happiness and good times: discounts, inclusions, free transfers; attractive dorms and swimming pools and beachside bars. It was pleasing to be on the edge of all the excitement, even if we couldn't take part.

'Well?' I asked Paul, when things began to quieten down and everyone else had chosen where they were going to stay. 'Where to now?'

'Walk into town, I suppose,' he said. He was leafing through our guidebook and had found a map of the town. 'It's not far. Let's find a park for a sit until we can start doorknocking. We only need one hotel or restaurant to say yes,' he went on, 'and then that's it. We're alright for a bit.'

It was a cheery thought, but the truth is we were unemployable. I was sickly thin, and my hair was past my shoulders and knotted. Paul always looked like he'd just woken up, at least until late afternoon, when his eyes finally brightened, and he came to life. For the entire trip – our hitchhike through Belgium, Germany, Austria and Italy – I marvelled at his capacity to be unprepared

5

and late. Our clothes had the look of sleep, too, and over-wearing. My shoes were ripped.

'Would you give me a job?' I asked, my arms open to display myself.

Paul gave me a once-over and inspected his own jumper, which was torn at the elbow and smeared with ferry grease. 'Why not?' he said. 'I'd take ya.' He smiled and tapped me on the arm. 'Fuck it, let's look around, anyway.'

'Yes, c'mon,' I said. 'Who wants a poolside barbecue?'

We picked up our packs. A solitary minibus was left on the dock, a bit of an old bomb: bumped around and scratched. A slim, middle-aged woman with long, curly brown hair stood next to it, holding a bundle of brochures but without any luck, it seemed. She had no customers, and we were the only ones left.

'Hello,' she said. 'Camping?'

'No, sorry,' I said.

'Where are you staying? Tell me.'

I was about to apologise again and walk away. Why stop if we didn't have any cash? But of course it was rude not to chat if people wanted to. 'We don't know,' Paul said. 'Somewhere near here, probably,' he added, making it up as he went. 'In town. We're looking for work, you know. Where should we start?'

The woman stepped close and handed us a brochure titled *Karousades Camping*. 'Here,' she said. 'You start here.' I opened it to behold pictures of a white beach and people drinking and eating on a shaded patio. What I noticed most, though, was that they looked healthy, contented, tanned and well fed. 'I can help you get work, too,' she offered, and I noticed her yellowish tan and smoker's wrinkles near her mouth. Small, friendly eyes. You got wary of the people hostels sent out; they were so perfectly

6

fresh and optimistic. But I trusted her. 'Where are you from?' she asked.

'Australia,' I said. I didn't add the whole story of really being from Iceland and England, too. 'He's from Scotland,' I added. 'Glasgow.'

'Are you together, then?'

'Aye,' Paul said, 'we're stuck together like chewing gum on a shoe.' The simile was his way of making a good impression.

She nodded in a neutral way as if to acknowledge Paul's efforts. 'Get in, then,' she said. 'I'm the only one left and I can see you've got nowhere to go and nothing better. You might as well come with me. Face it.'

She seemed to be saying that we all needed each other, whether we liked it or not. 'Oh, I don't think you understand,' I said.

She interrupted me before I could explain our situation. 'Are you worried you're the only ones with me? Don't be. No! I was late getting to the dock today. Normally, I have a full bus. You're lucky there's a spot. Very lucky. Get in. C'mon. Quick.' She slid open the door to the minibus. Inside were faux-leather seats that smelt of long drives and hot plastic.

'It's not that,' I said. I decided to just come out with it. 'Actually, we don't have any money. We can't pay you.'

The woman raised her eyes skywards. 'I didn't think so. It doesn't matter. You'll get work, and then you pay me.' She put out her hand. 'Helena,' she said. 'Get in, get in. I have to get back to cook breakfast. The guests are waking up. They'll be angry with me if there's nothing to eat. People are so impatient, even when they're on holiday. C'mon! This is taking too long.'

I turned to Paul. He was grinning with delight.

'Well?' she asked. 'Are you coming or not?'

'Yes, thank you,' I answered, and then repeated, 'Thank you.'

'Good. You sit in the front with me, long legs.'

Helena moved a clipboard and brushed a pile of receipts from the passenger seat and got behind the wheel. Then she turned the key to the ignition slowly, as though it needed to be at exactly the right angle and tempo to start the van; the engine wheezed, and we bounced off across the dock towards the gates and the road. She checked for traffic but behind us there was honking as we turned into the street. Helena sighed. 'You have to be careful driving in Corfu,' she said. 'So many crazy people these days!'

I watched the harbour stirring into life: trucks being reversed, delivery workers wheeling boxes on trolleys, and port labourers hosing driveways and delivery bays. The older men wore overalls or trousers hitched up over their stomachs in an old-fashioned way that reminded me of wartime pictures of my grandfather, who still wore his pants like that. The other side of the street was lined with ferry offices, car rental outlets and the first semi-industrial shops: fan belts, boat electricals, flooring suppliers and fitters.

It took a while to get out of town, which seemed to crowd the coastline, before thinning into suburbs of hotels, bars and boat yards, and then a wide bay with a necklace-like pebble beach, the first umbrellas and deckchairs. Behind us, in the side mirror, I watched the older part of town, with its Venetian facades, disappear, still lit orange-gold by the morning sun.

Helena handed me a packet of cigarettes. 'Take one out for me, as well,' she said. I passed her a cigarette and watched as she steered with her elbows while she lit up. She threw me the lighter.

'Relax now,' she said. 'It's an hour to Karousades. Today, relax. Sit in the sun. Sleep. Tomorrow, work.'

She looked in the rear-vision mirror. 'Everything okay?'

'Oh aye,' said Paul. 'Dandy!'

I believe that, by the time the road began to climb up into the hills of northern Corfu, I was already utterly spellbound. Perhaps Helena was a beneficent witch of some kind who knew how to trap young men who arrived on the island with no money and nowhere to stay. Maybe, at some point in the evening, she would send us into a deep sleep from which we wouldn't emerge until we were middle-aged.

That day, though, after I finished my cigarette, I closed my eyes but for a second and straight away felt giddy with tiredness – from the past weeks of travelling and trying to find work, and from the ship's movements. I opened my eyes again, preferring to watch the countryside go by. When I saw my eyes reflected in the glass, I felt that I recognised my father's, too, and remembered his nervous glances out of his car window when I'd met him in Reykjavík a month ago, just before this trip began.

Strange, I thought. Not strange that I was thinking about him, for our meeting had been such a big moment, as though a volcanic fissure had appeared in the ground beneath us. Rather, strange that I hadn't thought about him until now. My travels with Paul seemed to put him out of mind, like a jumper pushed to the bottom of a rucksack, and now the day I'd spent with him felt like such a long time ago, much more than a mere month. And yet, here he was, staring back at me in the translucent light of my own reflection. He knew how to spoil a nice day.

We cut inland; I caught glimpses of bays that cupped water clearer than the sky. In hills that extended north, we drove through small, cramped villages that were coming to life. The front doors of the houses opened onto the road, with only a brush-wide strip of lime to signal some kind of pavement. But the villagers seemed impervious to the traffic, or at least to Helena's van. Some carried large loaves of bread with a tiny white square of wrapping for the hand to hold. Others swept the empty car spots that doubled as balconies. From the way they held their brooms – determinedly; angrily, even – it looked like sweeping was a serious business.

'So different,' I said to myself.

'What's that?' asked Helena.

'It feels very different from where we've been so far. The other parts of Europe we've travelled through.'

'There's nowhere like Corfu,' she said proudly.

I knew from my father, from other Icelanders too, that islanders often thought like that. During our drive through Reykjavík, my father spoke about how special and unusual Iceland was, and that I should be proud to have been born there. It made *me* special. 'We are so few,' he said, referring to the inhabitants. 'And there's nowhere as beautiful as this country. What's more, there's no such thing as an Icelander who doesn't miss it when they're away. Every single day. You will, too.'

That was true of today, I noticed now, as I was suddenly inhabited by a strong awareness of *not* being in Iceland any longer and waited for Helena to make the case for the even greater specialness of Corfu. It wasn't to be. Her eyes stayed on the road, and she let the passing landscape and villages offer the supporting evidence for her claim.

Years later, when I was at university, I read Lawrence Durrell's description of first arriving in Corfu: he said it was where 'the blue really begins'. My tutor claimed that Durrell could beat all other writers with his prose style, and indeed there was no better phrase for how Corfu was that morning, and how right Helena was. It was as though you'd met the colour and its variants for the first time, and the whole of the island was somehow affected by it, made unique, even the hills and olive forests, strapped at their base with black netting, crisscrossed by tracks, sending shadows across the road.

The road steepened yet more; the corners sharpened. At the top of our climb, we could see across the northeast of the island and out to sea, where there were smaller islands and the Albanian coastline receded northwards. The landscape below was more varied: in some places, olive groves darkened the valley floors; in others, high cedar pines collected in ornamental clusters, Romanesque and opulent in their elegance. In one of the villages we passed, an older woman dressed entirely in black sat in a bus shelter that was only a bit bigger than her. If someone else had come along, they would have had to vie for room on the bench. She had one hand on a shopping cart, the other on her lap.

Our eyes met briefly as Helena slowed at the corner, and then she opened her eyes wider, I thought as a hello. I waved.

'Leave the women alone,' Helena joked. 'We have enough troubles.'

We passed through yet more impossibly narrow lanes with houses of lime-washed walls, slim balconies decorated with geraniums and bougainvillea, metal grilles on the ground-floor windows; I caught the smell of coffee and tobacco and bread. There were sun triangles in the village squares, where the houses didn't overlap enough to block the light. 'We're in Greece,' I said to Paul. It needed saying, to clear up the seeming improbability of it. Or the magnitude of our good luck.

I turned around. He was dozing. 'What was that?' he asked.

'I said, we made it to Greece. Can you believe it?'

He glanced outside. Two dogs were chasing the van with happy, unthreatening expressions until they gave up, somewhat confused by their failure to catch us. 'Not really,' he said. He closed his eyes, and I thought he'd gone back to sleep. 'Sometimes, life is very sweet,' he added, without opening them.

I wasn't going to question our luck. Helena wasn't a witch. She was a hard-working campground owner who needed business. My father wasn't in the window. He was still in Reykjavík, with his real family and busy work life that didn't involve long-lost love children turning up for a chat one early September morning. I closed my eyes and felt the sway of my tiredness again and breathed in the sweet air coming in from outside, of a new day that felt like a new me, and that belonged to a blue that was eternal but was also the very same blue I'd seen in my father's eyes, and in my own. *I will stay here for the rest of my life*, I told myself, contentedly.

Some moments later, Helena slowed the van and turned into a narrow driveway that dipped towards a small white house and a small field of tents. 'Go up to the village later. I'll tell you where to go.'

'Is that where we get work?' Paul asked.

'Not straight away,' Helena said. 'It's too late to get work today. Everything starts very early. I will tell you who to talk to. There is someone who will find you work. First, I will give you a tent. You can take a rest. Have some breakfast with the other guests. I'm going to make the pancakes. You sleep. Clean up. This afternoon, you go up to the village. There's lots of work in Corfu. Always work, work, work. I will tell you where.'

'Thank you,' I said. 'We're very grateful.' I was also hoping for a bit more information; I couldn't imagine getting work was as easy as walking up to the village. 'Is there someone we should talk to?' I asked. 'A restaurant?'

'Yes, of course there's a person,' said Helena, pulling up beside reception. 'A man. It's okay. We call him Pirate. He'll help you.'

'A pirate?'

Helena gave a short, smoker's laugh. 'Not really a *pirate*,' she said. 'That's just a fun name we give him, he gives himself. He owns the taverna. *A* taverna. There are lots of tavernas around here. He knows all the builders and farmers, and they go to him. He is very friendly. A friendly pirate! He will help you.'

I laughed along. There was no point second-guessing.

But there was more I wanted to express, and I didn't know how to put it. I could tell her again that we were grateful. Without knowing it, Helena had rescued us; she was a dream rescuer, I thought. Or a land spirit, as they were called in Iceland. But that was hardly something you said out loud. 'We're so lucky we met you,' I said. 'We were running out of options.'

'We were screwed,' added Paul. 'Totally.'

'You'll like it here,' Helena said, waving a hand in the air. We got out of the car, and she took a longer look at me. 'Don't fall asleep before you've had something to eat. You need food. I see it.'

'Whatever you say,' I said.

'The Pirate,' Helena said, smiling. 'He will fix it.'

13

2

An invitation to my sons

Corfu, September 2022

I will say that we did have a plan. I was eighteen, after all, and not eight. But it wasn't very advanced, even by the standards applied to the young male mind. Essentially: hitchhike through Europe until we were somewhere warm and get jobs when the money ran out. It got warm but we didn't find work. Our dire financial situation was partly why, in Corfu, my heart was so lifted by the sight of the bays and northern hills of the island, and by Helena's kind words. I experienced a sudden and total feeling of having arrived in the right place at just the right moment. I was seeing for myself that the world could be kind to strays.

And yet, despite that kindness, I couldn't be sure that our situation was recoverable, or that the man they called the Pirate would *fix it*. More probably, it was time to ask for help from our families to get home. Neither Paul nor I wanted that. Both of us were from single-parent families, and we hated the thought of asking for money from our mothers, who had enough of a struggle to pay the bills at home without being asked to send cash to retrieve us from Greece. We had no choice but to try the Pirate, and trust in Helena.

The events that followed are why I'm back now, all these years on. I've been in the village of Karousades for three weeks, since mid-August when I flew here from Brisbane, where I live and work as a writer and an academic. My wife, Olanda, and our sons – Finnur, who is sixteen, and Magnús, thirteen – arrive tomorrow.

I came ahead so that I could spend time in the village, to write. Yet life has been slow without my family. I see already that this story belongs to the boys, too, and that they will help me to make sense of why events that occurred when I was eighteen are still so important to me. I would dearly like them to take part in the telling of it.

My daily routine has been to write in the morning and walk and swim in the afternoon. The streets are empty and quiet from three in the afternoon until five-thirty, when the village's six shops – baker, butcher, grocer, chemist, convenience store and small school supplies shop – re-open and the streets wake to the sound of dinner pans being pulled out of cupboards, cats resuming feuds, wooden louvres swinging open with rusty creaks and whistles, buckets being washed out, patios being swept, the first scooters of the evening rushing between villages. A bit later, people step outside, seemingly just in case someone else has decided to. The dogs start barking until they realise it's just the neighbours looking around, just like every other afternoon.

The village is a few kilometres back from the coast, with none of the bars and restaurants of the seaside, which in any case aren't quite right for solo travellers. I've spent the evenings sitting contentedly, if also a bit lonely, on my apartment's slim balcony, watching the light fade over the hills of north Corfu until even the local quarry, with bright white stone that captures the last of the sun, dims and the streetlamps take over. In Brisbane, we live a busy family life, and so I always look forward to this kind of time on my own, imagining the quiet and the stillness. The time to write. When I get it, however, I start counting down the days until we're together again, pining for noise and commotion and even the arguments and irritations of everyday life: who should take the rubbish out, why no-one mentioned that it's our turn to wash the rugby jerseys, how it's possible that an empty ice-cream wrapper has sat under the passenger car seat for two weeks.

But I'm also a little nervous about asking them to join me. It all happened so long before I met Olanda, before the boys were born. Will they feel anything for the place? They've heard about it for years, but that doesn't mean they'll see it the way I do. Yes, it's a nice old Greek village. There's a pretty beach. Olives, sunshine. My memories. But the trip will offer more than those things, I hope. A chance to think about how we are together, and how we will be as the boys take their own first steps of adulthood.

The next day, I wake very early, before dawn, and go online to check their progress. They've landed in Heathrow and are waiting for their connecting flight to Corfu. They're exhausted and I'm wide awake, wishing they'd board their next flight straight away. But that's still a few hours off. I try to write and give up, and read instead until noon, when I drive to a supermarket in the next town, Roda, and stock up on drinks and snacks, and cold meats and bread for a late supper if they're hungry.

Back at the apartment, I message them again, making sure everything's still going smoothly and that they've made it between the Heathrow terminals, until Olanda has to give me the hint that my 'helping' is getting a bit much and I should just let them get to Corfu. *Everything is going great*, she texts. *We're tired and excited and a bit bored. We'll see you at the airport!*

My 'helpfulness' is not exactly a new thing. I have sometimes been over-protective of the boys, overly concerned about their safety. It's not in my nature to worry like this, but fatherhood found a side of me I hadn't encountered before. When the boys were smaller, I worried obsessively, especially about them being hurt by a car. We live in a complex of townhouses with its own driveway. The speed limit is ten kilometres an hour, but many of the residents drive much faster than that. I became known as the crazy guy who chased cars down the driveway, asking people to slow down. At night, after the boys were asleep in their beds, my mind raced between horrible scenarios until I could convince myself to stop worrying about things that, I assured myself, weren't going to happen.

I'm less edgy about cars now that the boys are older and more aware of their surroundings. But the roads on Corfu are something else. The island generally runs to a holiday pace, but with a driving style inspired by rallies, even in the narrow road in front of my apartment. I can't chase the locals down their own streets, I know that. My rental car, a Renault hatch, came patterned with scratches that must be inevitable: the man at the rental agency gave me a discount because of them, saying all the cars are like that by August, after a summer on narrow island roads. 'Don't worry if you scratch it some more,' he said. 'We won't notice.'

The drive from Karousades to Corfu Airport takes about an hour. When I finally leave for the airport, the sun is still high and blanches the leaves of the olive trees to silver. Near the quarry, the road winds high into the hills before falling down again towards the mid-east coastline, where it widens and sidles up to the first contours of the harbour until you find yourself in the middle of Corfu Town, with its ancient facades, rows of small shops and apartments, tight corners, and pretty, umbrella-lined restaurants and taverna. The airport is in town, too, on the fringes of the old streets.

Corfu has extraordinary landscapes, but it is not exactly one of those glamorous, postcard-perfect Greek islands that one calls to mind. It's more varied than that. There are wealthy pockets, such as the northeast of the island, which gets the nickname of Kensington-on-Sea, and it's also very popular with budget holidaymakers. The planes parked alongside the airport fence are Ryanair and Jetstar, and as I arrive in the airport grounds I see families dragging their suitcases beside the road rather than forking out for a taxi, looking hot and lost and annoyed with one another.

I park the car and wait inside. Though it's only been a few weeks since I've seen the boys, moments like this are still so oddly fresh and novel – as though we haven't seen each other in years and there's so much catching up to do, and I'll need to learn about them all over again. I've missed them terribly, I realise now.

'You made it,' I call out when at last they emerge through customs.

We hug. 'You're tanned!' Finnur says. 'And relaxed. Aren't you meant to have been writing? Dad, you've been sitting on the beach all day.'

'No, no, I have been writing, I promise. Work, work, work. That's all I've done. C'mon. Let's get out of here. We might have time for a swim.'

Outside, we cram into the scratched hatchback and begin our way to the village. I try not to point out too many things along the way. There's plenty of time for that: we'll be in Corfu for another two weeks. In their first minutes here, the boys notice the hills and olive groves that reach all the way down to the edge of the road. They marvel at the sea, reflecting hot white light, and the bays of the north as we climb towards the bends near the quarry. They say how much they love it. Already.

'At last,' Olanda says. 'We've made it to Corfu!'

'So good you're here,' I say.

It's lovely to hear them beginning to form their own impressions. But as we get closer to the village, I find myself issuing little warnings and disclaimers. 'Like I've said before, it's a *very* quiet village,' I begin. 'You know, just a few shops. Nowhere to go out to eat. For a lot of the day, there's not a soul in the street. Just a few old men sitting outside on benches in the square. More cats and dogs than humans.'

'Don't worry about that, Dad,' says Magnús. I feel his hand near my shoulder as he leans forward from the back seat. 'We can swim, right?'

'Yes. There's a beach just down the road. Astrakeri. But it's really quiet, too. One bar, some deckchairs for hire, paddle boats. Almost a suburban kind of beach.'

'Do you go there a lot?'

'Every day, pretty much. They're getting to know me. The barman's half-English. He likes to have a chat. Knows everyone. Makes a good burger, too.'

'There you go, boys,' says Olanda. 'Burgers on the beach.'

Actually, I love the slight scrappiness of Corfu; I shouldn't be apologising. Finnur joins in the task of reassuring me. 'It's fine!'

he calls from beside his brother. 'Better than fine. Look at this.' He's pointing at the view across to the channel, to the dusty-brown coastline of the mainland just a few kilometres away. 'It's incredible,' he says. And then, 'Are you alright, Dad? It's just us, remember. You don't have to *do* anything.'

'I know, I know,' I say, 'I'm going to have to relax, aren't I.'

The boys laugh at me, and the absurdity of it: that I'm bracing for some kind of letdown, on a Greek island in late summer, during school holidays, thousands of miles from early mornings, classes and assignments.

Still, there *is* one other matter that I'm keen to mention, a silly thing but one that I'd hate to colour their first impressions of the apartment. For the last few days in a row, one of the village cats has been bringing the gift of a dead mouse to my door. I'm dreading there will be one there when we get in. But in the silence of the final kilometre into the village, as we climb into the shadows of its step-like streets, I decide not to say anything. I'll let things unfold as they might, even the visiting cats and their presents.

We park a little way down from the apartment, next to a house-high retaining wall that fronts one of the oldest villas and where there's room for the hatchback, and drag the suitcases up the hill, disturbing the evening bird calls with the sound of plastic wheels grinding on the uneven bitumen. The elderly couple in the house next to the apartment see us through their open front door and wave, and I give a short introduction before we go up to the stairs. 'Ah, they're here at last,' I imagine them saying to each other. Or, 'They really *do* exist, just like he said.'

No new mouse at the door today. Even the deathly smell near the doorway, which has come to accompany these gruesome donations, has been eased by a breeze and the magical fragrances of early evening in Greece: the herbs being cooked in the kitchens around us, the cedar and olive trees, the salty air rising from the coast, scooter emissions, grills burning.

It's a modest but attractive apartment – breezy with French windows and a compact kitchen, two good-sized bedrooms. The first thing the boys do is connect their phones to the wi-fi; it's not the only thing on their minds, but I can see they're relieved that the internet is fast. They have their world with them wherever they go, and perhaps half or a quarter of a mind reserved for what isn't here in front of them. I'm glad it wasn't like that when I was their age. Escape was still possible; remoteness felt real and part of what it meant to get away. But as soon as they're connected, the boys join me and Olanda on the balcony and tonight, for the first time in about a month, I have company while I sip on a glass of the local rosé, which is crisp but also has a hint of methylated spirits.

'Alright?' I ask Olanda.

'Kári, it's stunning.' Not the wine, although she doesn't seem to mind its cheery medicinal tang. She's gazing at the view over the rooftops, down to a valley that separates Karousades from the next cluster of houses, the neighbouring village of Antiperni.

'This used to be the main town in the north,' I say. 'But you can see that's all changed.'

'I love it,' she says.

'Quite run down, I guess,' I add.

'Yes. Perfect.'

It's a bit late to drive to the beach for a swim. Instead, the four of us sit on the balcony until dark, snacking on the cold meats and feta cheese and bread I bought earlier. As Olanda says, it's perfection. As the boys struggle to keep their eyes open, I hear them calculate that they've been travelling for nearly two days; for the last fifteen minutes of the evening they run over complicated theories about the optimum time to go to bed to ensure a maximum sleep-in in the morning. 'Right now,' says Magnús, at the conclusion of their talk.

The next morning, it's ten before we leave for our first walk together through the village. The apartment is at the top of a hill, so our stroll along the main street slopes down to the first of two small town squares, one with a post office and medical centre. The second is where the bus sometimes stops but quite often doesn't bother to, and where the old men sit on what seem to be specially made benches that are just thin enough to keep them from being hit by passing cars. They wave to us as we walk towards the church, the butcher and grocer, and other empty shops.

At a small crest there is a taverna, a proud and comfortable little restaurant with a glass front and red steel security grilles. Inside are a collection of tables that look as though they've only just stopped being used: there are bottles and plates and glasses, but no order. A feeling of sudden closure, some shock that hasn't been remedied with a proper tidy-up or emptying out.

The restaurant is divided by a high bench into two areas, the kitchen with its barbecue grill and its pots and pans, and a service area framed by blue walls that are decorated with shelves of old bottles, postcards and photographs, and a large, dust-covered TV in the corner.

On the bench, beside a vase of bright plastic flowers, sits a framed picture of a man with long grey hair and a thick moustache, holding his hands resignedly or perhaps merrily in the air, a gesture that could say many things: *yes, take my photo;*

yes, you are welcome here, my friend; yes, it's time to eat and drink. Sit down, sit down. Join me. There's no hurry. Let's talk. Let's drink. It's my own wine. I grew it. Yes, sit with me and talk. Those were the kinds of things he used to say.

'That's the Pirate?' Finnur and Magnús ask in unison.

'That's him,' I say. And so the story I've invited them to hear, a gift of sorts, has now reached the front step of a taverna where things had eventually come to a head.

3

The Pirate

Corfu, September 1990

At high school, I'd been a very analytical student. But when, at the end of my last year, it was time for me to travel on my own for the first time, I found I was more willing to allow things to unfold at their own pace and direction. I did reflect on the people I met and the things that happened to me in a journal that I kept, but I wasn't seeking to plan or direct my travels. I didn't understand this very well, but it was as though travelling on one's own insisted on a kind of surrender to the invitations of the road. They were so rich and varied, after all, even if they also sometimes brought troubles.

After we got to the campground and Helena showed us our tent, I took a long shower in a open-air wooden cubicle, in water that was a little warmer than outright cold. It had only been two nights since we'd had a proper place to sleep and get clean, but the soap and water on my skin made me feel as though I was emerging from a long tunnel. I put on a cleanish pair of jeans and T-shirt and walked barefoot back to the tent. The ground was dusty and soft, as if it were near a dried riverbank, and crackly with semi-submerged thin roots.

After Paul had his shower, we joined the other campground guests at the patio. They noticed us and smiled and went back to their breakfasts, planning their days, reading maps and guidebooks. Helena's pancakes. Everything was lovely, with the usual backpacker's assembly of languages, couples, a slightly older solo traveller, a group of four friends who looked like they'd known each other since school, and a pretty girl with black hair, who stood slipping an apple into her day bag, and wore an expression of not being sure whether that was the right thing to do.

After breakfast, I borrowed a copy of *Wuthering Heights* from the reception library and spent the morning reading. When we ambled up to the village in the afternoon, following Helena's instructions, I brought its ghostly perspective with me. The houses seemed to shape in, like the entry to a castle, or a gorge where the walls narrowed. Soon, we were surrounded by side lanes, and shadows, and shuttered windows. Parked at odd angles, cars and scooters suggested life, a population, but there was no-one around. You merely felt their presence behind windows, half-open doors. But it wasn't bleak. The street was overlooked by second-floor balconies decorated with flowers. They weren't wide enough to sit on; they were more decorative than that, like long, painted eyelashes.

My eyes adjusted to the pace of the village, and I began to notice that, actually, all sorts of things were happening. A bakery, with a front window half-above and half-below ground level, was closing for the day. Another small shop, barely more than a front room, was selling coffee, drinks and cigarettes. Further up, a shoe seller's window; on our right, the glass doors of the first taverna and a bench that marked the bus stop.

The taverna didn't seem to have a name: there was an Amstel

sign, and a Greek flag hanging loosely from the balcony above wide front windows, but no menu or opening hours. 'This must be it,' I said. 'I can't see anywhere else with a bench out the front.'

'I am not an expert in Greek tavernas,' Paul confessed, modestly.

I put my face to the front window and peered in. No-one there, no lights on. But definitely a restaurant. A single room, not very spacious, but cosy rather than cramped. A tall wooden bench ran most of the width of the room, separating a dozen tables from the kitchen. An open grill behind the bench nearest the window, black pots and pans hooked onto the back wall. In the dining area, a wall shelf displaying a long line of empty bottles coloured dark blue and green; a piece of timber that appeared to be from a boat; speakers; in one corner, a television on a raised platform.

'No-one,' I said to Paul, and stepped back.

He took a turn at the glass. 'What do you call *him*, then?'

'What?' I joined him. The Pirate. I gasped and pulled back. 'Shit. I didn't see him.' The man was sitting at the table closest to the kitchen, on the phone. In the shadows, wearing black, not moving. But definitely a living person.

'Knock, you idiot,' Paul said, and did so himself before I could stop him. The man in the shadows didn't move. 'I'll knock again. He didn't hear me.'

'No, no, wait. Why the hell do you think he didn't hear you? He's right there! We don't want to upset him. Can't you see, he's on the phone.'

'How would we upset him? It's a taverna. We're here to go to the taverna, for Christ's sake.' Paul held out his hands. 'We want taverna,' he said, raising one, 'taverna here,' he concluded, lifting the other.

'We're not exactly customers, though, are we.' I saw that the man still hadn't moved. Still no lights. It was as though he was a plastic model, part of the décor. Maybe he hadn't heard us, after all. 'Go on, then,' I said. 'Knock again. Might as well.'

Paul banged hard on the glass. It wobbled a little, and at last a reaction. A frown from the man. 'He looks angry,' I said. 'Damn.'

Paul pressed his face to the glass. 'He looks dead.'

'Why hasn't he moved?' I asked.

'I mean, he's on the phone,' Paul said. 'He must be alive. Let's stand here until he's finished.'

'Alright.'

We turned our backs to the glass to give him some privacy while he finished his phone call. It was past five o'clock and people were stepping from their houses into the street. It would get cooler soon, I thought. A scooter passed us; the rider stared and then nodded. '*Yassas*,' he said. We waved.

'It seems friendly here,' I said.

'Beautiful,' Paul said. 'Rustic. Charming,' he continued, drawing out each word. 'Crumbling. Ancient. Ruinous.'

'Stop it. Do you feel like you're being watched?'

'From the minute we left the campground. But look at us. I'd be suspicious of us if we walked into our village.'

Paul meant Aviemore, the resort town in the Scottish Highlands where we'd met and worked together and first began talking about travelling on the Continent. It was where he'd told me about the problems in Glasgow that he'd fled and that made him want to get away even further.

'People kept an eye on us there, too,' I said.

'Don't mind it,' Paul said. 'Maybe we should go for a walk. Have a look around. We're being weird standing here like this.

I feel like a criminal. A miscreant. He could be on the phone for hours. I want to see the pretty wee village.'

Before we could go, the sliding glass door rumbled open. 'What is it?' The Pirate's head appeared while his body stayed behind the door, in the dark. 'I'm not open,' he said. 'Fuck off.'

I put out my hand. 'You must be the Pirate,' I said.

He didn't take it. 'Do you hear me? I'm closed. Fuck off.'

I lowered my hand and stared at him in amazement, paralysed by his greeting and by his looks. It was no wonder people called him the Pirate, for there could not have been a more pirate-like head in existence. An oval-shaped face with thick cheeks. A crooked nose. Terribly dark eyes that bulged but were also hazy, and angry, as closed for business as his taverna. In fact, it was a face to match his establishment: shadowy, uncertain, from another time, too. And something weirdly welcoming as well, as though 'fuck off' had a hint of hospitality in it.

'Well?' he said. 'What is it?'

'Yes,' I said.

He blinked slowly. 'Yes, what?'

'Helena sent us. From Karousades Camping. She said you have work.'

'Oh?'

'We came to see if you had any work. Jobs.' I made digging and hammering actions with my hands to illustrate.

The Pirate's expression didn't change. 'What are you doing that for?' he asked wearily. 'I know what *work* is. Do you think I'm stupid? Do you think I can't speak English? Are *you* stupid?'

'Sorry,' I said.

'He is stupid,' Paul said, trying to raise a laugh.

The Pirate inspected us as we stood there. I felt acutely aware of our clothes. But he didn't seem to notice, and now I wondered if it struck him as a good thing that we weren't well dressed or prosperous-looking. His eyes rested on my face and hair. Finally, something like a smile appeared, although directed inwards, perhaps – at his own thoughts.

'Okay,' he said, pointing at me. 'You. Eight.' He pointed at the door and then the ground in front of it. 'Here. Eight. Then, we see about work.'

'Thank you,' I said. 'I'll be here.'

The Pirate nodded and pulled the glass door closed. Inside, he raised his hand in a shooing motion and returned to his seat in the corner, with his phone and cigarettes and ashtray. 'Go!' he yelled. 'I'm busy, can't you see!'

We wanted to obey but couldn't decide which way to walk – whether to go further into the village or straight back to the campground. We took a few steps out of the village, changed our minds. Stopped and turned to each other, and then laughed, relieved and still a bit shocked. 'We can have a wander around the village, can't we?' I asked. 'That won't upset him?'

'Aye, we can,' said Paul, 'now that we're not shitting ourselves.'

We walked past the taverna again, making sure to avert our gaze; even Paul kept his eyes forward. The main road through the village dipped and then began a second ascent to the church and the town square. The buildings were unified less by colour than by tone: white, light blue, yellow and pink buildings all looked like they'd been painted on the same day twenty years before, although *faded* would be the wrong word – it seemed fairer to say that the paint had sunk in properly. At their base, many of the houses were lime-coated, with the result that the village as a whole felt stripey in a celebratory way, like a collection of flags.

'How about that, then,' said Paul. 'Do I not look trustworthy?'

'It's just the job,' I said. 'He only needs one of us.'

'Do you think he wants someone he can slide through the drainage grills?'

'I'm not that thin.'

The last climb in the village was buttressed on the right by a high retaining wall, painted yellow, above which were the more affluent homes – built in the style of French manor houses, with wide, classical facades and tall windows; dense, shinning vines entwined the guttering and dark gates. Though beautiful, the mansions seemed less cared for than the smaller homes in the village, in the way of inherited houses that across the generations become too expensive to maintain. They implied a more prosperous time in the past.

Maybe that was the case with the Pirate, too, I mused. If not a prosperous past, what was the *life before* that existed in the taverna, concealed by the tablecloths and bottles and darkness? He didn't seem friendly enough to be a restaurateur. Or maybe Paul and I were just too shabby to be customers. To be worth impressing.

As we returned to the campground, Helena saw us from her office and waved through the window. 'Did you find him?' she asked.

Paul was still in a bit of a huff. 'He wants Kári to come back in the morning. He doesn't need me, it would appear.'

'He will, he will,' she said, not acknowledging his resentment. 'There's always more to do. Did he say what the job is?'

'No,' I said. Maybe there was something odd in that, and in the way he'd weighed up my suitability by looking me over. 'Is he okay?' I asked. 'I mean, he seems a bit ...'

'Oh, yes, the Pirate is okay.' Helena shrugged her shoulders philosophically. 'A bit different, but okay.'

'Kári thinks he's being sold into sex slavery,' Paul muttered under his breath. 'As if that would work!'

'Do you want a beer?' Helena asked.

'Um, I'm not sure,' I said.

'It's okay, pay me later.'

'Thank you, then. Yes.'

Helena stepped out with two tall bottles of Amstel. 'See,' she said as she handed them to us, 'the gods are smiling on you today.'

I opened my bottle and took a sip. 'Are you having one?' I asked.

'Not yet,' Helena said. 'Too much to do. Why don't you sit down over there,' she said, pointing at a circle of log chairs near a blackened fire pit. 'Everyone will be coming back soon, and you'll have company. Then you can hear more about the island and make your own plans. It's good to listen to others.'

We did as we were told. It was a luxurious time of day; the sun was behind the hills but still present in reflections and a dart-like gold that twitched on the leaves. In places where the shadows fell, the groves became purple rather than evening-dark, as though the changing hours released centuries of olive dye from the ground. It was very still: I noticed that the crickets were louder than the cars and scooters that occasionally drove past. I sighed with contentment, even if the promise of a day's work for one of us didn't solve our problems.

I was thinking about the Pirate; Helena seemed to have

confidence in him, and I wanted to put my faith in her and even him. But our first meeting wasn't very encouraging. 'The Pirate,' I said to Paul. 'What an act!' Surely that was the only way to interpret his bluster and rudeness. He was playing the part of a grumpy old seaman.

'The biggest pile of shite I ever saw,' said Paul, nodding.

'Imagine having to call yourself a Pirate just to get the tourists in,' I chortled.

'He's a *character*.'

I gave it some thought. 'Then again, maybe we just lack imagination,' I said. Neither of us could really claim to know how to identify a pirate, if we saw one.

'Or he lacks reality.'

'How old do you think he is?' I asked.

'I would say, oh, between thirty-five and forty-five.'

'Can you be more precise, please.'

'In my experience, drinkers with his commitment level are very difficult to guess. Some pickle young, some turn into withered prunes. Your man there in the taverna hasn't had a dry night since he was a wee one. I know it when I see it. There's a thousand of those guys on the streets of Glasgow, and they all have a funny nickname and some story or other to go with it, but it's all done to get someone to buy them a drink.'

'Except he's not really pickled or pruned,' I said. 'Somewhere in between. I mean, he looks okay if he's forty-five.'

'Well, he's no pirate, in my expert assessment,' Paul concluded. 'Rude bastard, though. I'll say that much. Telling us to fuck off like that. How dare he!'

'It doesn't matter. There might be other options. I'll do the job tomorrow; you have a look around for what else is going.'

Probably, Paul was right, and we'd just met a character-actor. But I'd seen something else. Openness that lay beneath the surface of his rudeness. After all, he said to come back. At that time in my life, with things the way they were, that was enough of a reason to do so.

Other people who were staying at the campground were getting in from their day trips around the island. Mostly, it was couples and pairs, but the pretty girl with black hair I'd seen pocketing an apple in the morning walked down the driveway on her own. There was no reason to take note of it, but both Paul and I did. 'I thought you had a broken heart,' Paul said.

'You're looking, too.'

'I am as free as a bird,' he said. 'You are an albatross that canna take off from the cliff face. You are restricted.'

Paul was referring to the fact that, just before we left Scotland, I'd had an unhappy break-up. The girl I'd been seeing had decided that I was like other Australians she'd met, a flight risk who would leave at any moment. She'd broken it off and gone back to an ex-boyfriend before I had the chance to go first, which she was convinced that I was going to do. Paul was right when he said I was weighed down by that. 'I'm starting to hate it when you talk in metaphors,' I said, rather than agree with him.

But there was more to it than that. As I'd felt in the morning, while we drove with Helena from the port, the sensation of having reached a stopping point in our travels, like a sheltered bay, also brought me closer to the afternoon I'd spent with my father. It hadn't been good and I could feel the sting of it now. But for the first time, I also wondered how he had coped with our meeting, after we'd said goodbye. I'd assumed he was relieved it was over, but maybe I was unfair in thinking that – making assumptions, as we were doing about the Pirate.

'Is my language not to your liking?' Paul went on, interrupting my thoughts. 'Here she comes. Isn't this when you get your *I'm so sensitive and interesting* look on?'

'Shut up or go to the tent,' I said, laughing. 'She's not going to want you around, that's for sure. With your *language*, as you call it.'

Despite our magnetic presence at the fire pit, the girl avoided the area completely and went to her tent, and we were left with our own reflections for a bit longer. Almost unbelievably, everything about our travels seemed to have changed. Like the glass door of the Pirate's taverna, good luck had shuddered open, and we had everything we needed: food, a tent, beer and cigarettes, and maybe even dinner, if Helena's generosity extended that far. And, at the end of the day's work tomorrow, actual money!

Others joined us by the fire pit, and just before dark Helena came down, too. She asked for help to get the fire going and then went back to the building to set up a grill. There were a few bedrooms in the building, but they were small and uninviting, and all of the other guests were sleeping in tents. A young American couple said hello. The woman, Bella, was a teacher; her husband, Joe, a fireman. They were from the Midwest and very different sizes, he tall and muscular, she mouse-like and sweet, but they wore the same settled smile, as though the world would only ever smile back.

I did so now, as we talked about their travels. They listed all the places they'd seen. It was their first time abroad and they wanted to see the whole world. After Greece, they were going to Asia and the Pacific, and then Australia before they flew to California. They'd spent today on scooters touring the island. They said we should do that. It was so much fun. Their favourite beaches were on the far west of the island, where the cliffs were high and some of the bays could only be reached by boat. I liked hearing their stories, and I marvelled at how orderly their travels were. Was I jealous of them? Yes, I thought, I definitely was. What on earth were we doing, bumbling our way through the Continent, our fate dependent on the goodness of strangers?

'Oh, no, I love it,' said Bella when I expressed some of these misgivings about our mode of travel. 'It's so free. If only we could do that, we would.' She turned to Joe. 'Wouldn't we, honey?' Joe nodded. 'Don't you see – it means you can't predict what'll happen. It's liberating!'

She was right, though it only took someone with enough money and maybe a bit too much organisation behind them to see it. Bella said she and Joe had been planning their itinerary in detail for two years. She could tell us exactly where they'd be in two weeks, three weeks, a month. She was very polite but also frank. She said it'd be wrong to dismiss what she was saying just because she was watching our efforts from a safe distance. She wanted to convince me that we were lucky to be directionless. I nodded and felt the relief of talking to someone other than Paul, who I think was thinking the same about me.

The girl with black hair came out of her tent and sat on one of the logs. She had a small guitar with her and, after she'd said hello to everyone, she plucked the strings gently rather than speaking much. 'It was a gift from a friend,' she explained when she noticed me listening to her play. 'I'm still learning quite a bit.' She kept hitting off notes and her rhythm was oddly syncopated. But she didn't appear to mind that she was blundering, and she was louder and more confident in her playing as she went on with it. All the same, I felt the others around the fire were grateful when she put the guitar down at her side.

'I'm Michelle,' she said to me. 'I'm from Geneva.'

'Thanks for the music,' I said, enthusiastically.

'Do you like them?'

'Sorry?'

'The band I was playing. Do you like them?'

I had no idea that she'd been playing a song. 'Oh, yeah,' I lied.

'Can you believe they've only had one hit?'

'It's weird, isn't it. What's it called again?' I asked. I didn't recognise the song at all.

'Oh, c'mon, you haven't forgotten. "Take On Me".'

Her looks were Italian: in the firelight, her eyes seemed as dark as her black hair, her skin olive-coloured. Her story was that she had left Switzerland during her university summer holidays, intending to travel through all of Greece, including a few of the islands. But when she got here, she didn't want to leave Corfu, and now she'd been staying at the campground for three weeks. She didn't think she was going to see anywhere else, not this time.

'That's okay, that's great, better even,' said Bella, and I thought her support for Michelle's stationary approach seemed to contradict her earlier admiration of our wanderings.

'Yeah, absolutely okay,' said Joe, the fireman husband. 'If you like it here, why rush around? We're probably doing too much, but we don't know if we'll ever be able to afford to come to Europe again. And *time*, you know. If we're blessed with children. Then, you don't travel, not like this.'

'It's not very exciting of me,' said Michelle. 'But I love it here so much. I don't want to leave.'

'What makes it so special?' I asked.

'I don't know if I can say it all in words,' she said. 'I like islands.'

A young Austrian man called Felix joined us. He knew

Michelle and the American couple. He said he was on leave from his compulsory military service and had been working as a builder's labourer on the island's construction sites. 'Everyone is building here,' he said. 'It's all villas for rich Germans and English. You will get work. Don't worry.'

Felix was one of those guys who started smiling before you'd finished your sentence, as though all ideas would end in laughter, even though they didn't. It made me feel uneasy about him, but I was tired, and I assumed I was wrong. He was handsome in an enviably easy way, with blond curly hair and a wide-mouthed, bright-eyed smile that instantly improved the atmosphere in the group. I yawned and reminded myself that there was no need to work him out, or the Pirate, or my father, even. There was nothing wrong with looking at a fire and the flight of insects under the trees. But Felix wanted to be friends and kept talking to me. It felt like he was trying to tell me something indirectly, maybe that there was something between him and Michelle, I couldn't tell for sure.

I got more tired and began withdrawing into my thoughts. I wanted to keep up with the conversation and not drift. But I felt the weeks of being on the road suddenly collecting at my feet, and I couldn't concentrate on what people were saying. I didn't want to be the quiet one in the group, so I stood up and said goodnight.

Helena spotted me on my way back to the tent. 'Here,' she called, and brought down a plate of grilled meatballs and salad and bread. I thanked her and ate my meal outside. I heard the others heading up to the dining area, and I enjoyed not only the food but also the most sumptuous feeling of solitude, the type that comes from being pleasantly on the margins of others' activities, but also staying partly connected – the feeling that storytellers

often experience as happiness. When I finished my food, I took
my paper plate to the campfire, now unattended, threw it into the
flames, and climbed into the tent to sleep.

4

What we tell our children

Corfu, September 2022

The man in the picture on the dividing bench in the untidy, discarded taverna looks quite a bit friendlier than the Pirate as we first met him. 'It's hard to believe it, I know, but he frightened us,' I say to the boys as we head back to the apartment. 'He was hard to read, too. But we couldn't go back to the ferry, or on to Athens. We were already stuck, in a way.'

'Stuck on a Greek island,' says Finnur, shaking his head. 'You must have been so unhappy about that.'

'Wasn't the ticket valid?' Magnús asks. As often, checking the logic of things, and making sure I've got the facts straight.

'Yes,' I say, 'but the ferry only came twice a week. We didn't have enough money to get back to the ferry terminal, not even enough for the local bus ticket. And if we did, what were we going to do in Athens with no money? We had to stay and see what came next.'

Magnús nods but I sense a little doubt. 'It sounds like a folk tale to me,' he says. 'An old lady who you kind of thought was like a witch rescues you from the harbour and brings you to see a pirate who is scary and mean. You're too poor to refuse his help. So, you're imprisoned on a Greek island. Banished until you can make good. It's a computer game.'

'I see what you mean. That's how it happened, though. All true.'

I feel the bouncing weight of Magnús's arm on mine while we walk. He likes to lean against me like this. 'It's a shame it's such a mess,' he says. 'They should keep the taverna going. Re-open it.'

'It wouldn't feel the same,' Finnur suggests.

'Never mind,' I say. 'Let's get some brunch and have a swim. We'll come back another day, before we leave. Get some pics of us together.'

Already, with the boys here, being back and looking at the taverna in its present state feels much more purposeful. I've walked past it almost every afternoon on my way to the beach. The front of the restaurant was starting to become just another building that I crossed. Even the Pirate's photo was losing its life, like the artificial flowers it sits beside. How magical it is that, with the boys at my side, the room comes back to life, and the Pirate, too. He's telling us *all* to 'fuck off' this time, although he would never have been so rude to a family that chanced upon his taverna. After all, he was a businessman as well as a pirate. He would have smiled and opened his arms wide, and set aside a special table beside the windows.

We collect our things from the apartment. After they've packed their bags, the boys ask me about what happened before I got to Corfu. How it was that Paul and I ended up being here. I begin by telling them a little about how I met Paul in Aviemore. 'He was from Glasgow and left there because there wasn't any work. He was meant to be sending money home. But he wasn't ever going to manage it. It just wasn't like him to settle down and work hard or stick to a plan. I met his family once or twice and they all knew it about him, too.

'We started on the same day, and I liked him straight away. We were made to do a two-day induction course. It was us two and one other guy, and we weren't taking it very seriously. Paul was so bored he started answering everything the instructor said in a weirdly formal way, in his heavy Glaswegian accent. Things like, "By turns remarkable and efficient," or, "Very reasonable in the circumstances," and, "That is surely the appropriate way to perform a duty of that kind."'

'The instructor must have loved that,' says Finnur.

'He was fine, actually. He ended up going along with it. That's usually the best thing to do with cheeky students.'

Finnur knows I'm also talking about him, but he lets me go on. 'Anyway, Paul had always wanted to travel. I think he saw me as a bit of a ticket out of Scotland. His family didn't have the money for it. My mum didn't have any money either, but she travelled anyway. I guess that was the difference. I was used to moving around. He liked that about me: how I was already used to the idea of travel. I think it reassured him that it could be done. He was very Scottish, or what I thought of as Scottish and loved. He took the piss a lot. Knew how to have fun. But he didn't care one bit about money. He'd happily spend all he had in a night, if he could. "It'll be alright, Kári," he always said.'

'Great Scottish accent,' says Magnús, giggling.

I tell them about the bumpy journey across Europe that followed. Days spent on the roadside hoping for a ride. Being picked up by the police and taken back into town, told to avoid hitching and to catch a train, instead. The troubles of cheap travel, and an innocence and trust that I find almost impossible to imagine now. But also, the sequence of wonders we encountered as we journeyed south through Germany, Austria and Italy. The feeling of ever more openness that came after the Alps, as the air warmed and the food was cheaper and seemingly more luxurious as well. Waiting for a ferry in Brindisi, our last cash spent on two deck fares to Athens and a carton of cigarettes that was about to go missing.

'Did you smoke a lot?' asks Magnús.

'Everyone did. Well, everyone who worked in hospitality.'

'I'm glad you don't smoke now,' he adds, just in case I'm thinking of it.

'Don't worry,' I say. 'The last time I smoked was the cigar I had when you were born.'

'No, you had that one when you turned forty,' says Finnur. 'At Noosa.'

'You remember that? Nine years ago, then.'

'Nearly ten,' says Magnús.

In the past, I've given them a simplified version of what happened next, in the almost fairy tale, as Magnús puts it. The computer game. A version that wasn't so much about me as it was all about a pirate. *A real one*, I always insisted. *Most certainly real*. For, if he was the real thing, then it made perfect sense that things didn't end up going smoothly. How could they if pirates were involved?

'But you're okay,' I remember Finnur asking, wide-eyed and scared for me. He must have been seven or eight at the time.

'Yes.'

'Because you're here now, telling the story.'

'Exactly.'

I was right there, safe at home in suburban Brisbane, with them, so I must have got away. *Escaped*. Wasn't that the best word to use, to describe getting away from the perils of piracy?

'Was there a ransom? Knives?' Magnús asked.

'Nothing like that, but he always made sure we knew he was a pirate,' I said, ambiguously, leaving the rest to their imaginations.

'How do you know for sure, then?' Magnús asked, sensing that I was holding something back.

'For starters, he looked like a pirate,' I said. 'You know, black moustache, long black hair tied back, broken nose, crooked smile. All the pirate essentials.'

'What's a crooked smile?'

'Like this,' I said. I tilted my head and made a sidelong grimace.

The boys cackled. 'Anyone could do that!' Finnur yelled. They both tried their best to pull their smiles to one side.

'He was more piratey than that, though,' I assured them. 'You two just look like you've got toothache.'

'I bet he *was* a pirate,' Finnur concluded, nodding to his brother, insisting on his agreement, too.

Now that the boys have just seen a picture of the actual Pirate, I fear they'll also reach the end of the caricature, and the simplification of the past that caricatures allow. The fairy tale dissolves?

As if prompted by my realisation, Finnur begins another line of questioning. 'But you came here straight from Iceland?' he asks. 'I mean, straight after you'd been there to see your dad.'

'More or less. It took us a few weeks to get here. We weren't very good at hitchhiking. Maybe it's more accurate to say we stood

45

on the sides of roads through Europe. But enough people stopped. Usually middle-aged men.'

'They felt sorry for you?'

'Probably. Recognised our blind stupidity. Wanted some company.'

He waits for a moment. 'I know you've told us before, but what happened in Iceland? With your dad? Do you mind telling us again?'

I catch him shooting a conspiratorial glance at Magnús that makes me think they've been trying to remember the different pieces of that moment for themselves, maybe even this morning. They might feel a little embarrassed that they don't remember it better for themselves.

'I don't mind at all,' I say. 'You must know most of it, though, don't you? I mean, I've even written about it.'

They have copies of my books, and the fuller story contained in them, although I'm not sure they've ever made it past the opening pages. 'Just tell us, Dad,' Magnús says. 'We're not on a reading holiday.'

In any case, a telling reflects its own moment, and my listeners are changing very quickly at the moment. With it, their understanding.

When they were younger, and they heard about the Pirate and other adventures that pre-dated their lives, the boys often seemed to be slightly in disbelief at the shape of the world as it existed before they came along. It was true of the stories that my mum told them, as well, and that I would fill out. She used to look after the boys twice a week, until they were old enough to look after themselves for an hour or two after school, before Olanda and I got home.

They knew Mum so well, but not very thoroughly, and so a kind of magical confusion appeared in their eyes when they learnt things about how she was as a young woman – her adventurous spirit that led her to travel the world, and eventually live in Iceland, where she met my father. Of course, they understood that she hadn't always been a grandmother, and that she must have had another life once, one that didn't involve them or me. But that doesn't fully explain photos like the one I show them now on my laptop, of a beautiful young woman with long black hair down to her waist, standing in a street in Reykjavík, pregnant with me. It's both her and not her, and almost impossibly different. The picture is real, though, I assure them. It even has *Reykjavík, 1972* written on it. Direct evidence.

She moved to Iceland in 1970, at the end of travels she made across the world when her marriage ended, from Australia to Japan and the Soviet Union and England. When she got to Reykjavík, she felt like she'd come home, even though, or perhaps because, it was so different from anything she'd experienced before. The remoteness and isolation of an island in the North Atlantic excited her. And, I think, offered healing for her wounded heart. She had endured a bad ending to her marriage in Australia. In Iceland, such a gentle and embracing island back then, she found the solace and quiet she needed.

'That's when she met my father, your grandfather,' I say. 'But I can't really tell you all that much about him. I only met him a few times.' The boys never met him; my father died in 2010 and was very unwell for some years before that. 'You do remember that he was already married and had five kids.' They nod. 'He was already taken,' I add with a touch of feigned melodrama.

'But he didn't marry Amma?' Magnús asks. They've always used *Amma*, the Icelandic for *grandmother*, for Mum.

'How could he, Magnús,' Finnur says, without any criticism in his voice. 'He was already married.'

'That's right,' I say. 'They couldn't be together. But she fell pregnant with me and that's how come I was born in Reykjavík. We didn't leave until much later. We moved to England when I was ten and then to Brisbane when I was fourteen.'

'You were a year older than me,' says Magnús.

'Correct.'

'Brilliant maths,' adds Finnur, laughing. 'A genius.'

I have never wanted the boys to think ill of my father, even if he had his failings. I don't like blame narratives; they can trap the storyteller inside their anger. But I feel the boys have a right to know what happened, even if I have to repeat the details at moments like this. 'I think he was a loving family man,' I say, 'and I think he loved his wife, but he also loved Amma. You can see it was a difficult situation for everyone. Eventually, Amma really just had to leave. She probably wanted something different for me than being a secret child in a little country like Iceland. She was doing her best.'

'No-one knew who you were?' Finnur asks.

It's a funny way to put it, but he's half right. 'Well, *I* knew who I was. Other people did, too. I mean, I was *me*, right? But only Amma and I knew who *he* was. That was the big secret, I suppose. The bit that had to stay between us.'

'How often did you meet him?' Finnur asks.

'He did visit when I was small,' I said. 'But he was nervous that I'd recognise him in the street and call out to him. So, he used to visit at night, when I was asleep. There was a time when I was seven that he came to see us while I was still up. He gave me some money for a soft drink. That made me feel happy, because it was a treat that had come from him.'

Finnur nods. 'And you decided to go and see him when you were seventeen?'

'In 1990, during my gap year after high school. I'd been working in Aviemore – where I met Paul – but before he and I started our travels together, I flew to Reykjavík and called my dad. It didn't go very well. We went for a drive and he was nice enough. He was trying, I could tell. His natural tendency was to be kind to others. I could see that about him. But it was a hard day for me, because he also made it clear that he couldn't be part of my life. He said it would jeopardise his marriage. His children would judge him for what he'd done. You can understand why he wasn't able to be a father to me. He thought he had to choose between me and them.'

Finnur gazes at me in disbelief. 'I can't understand why he wouldn't want to be in your life,' he says.

It's a large thing for him to digest, as it was for me when it happened. There's a part of me that doesn't want him and Magnús to have to hear about it at all, for I don't want to burden them with my relationship with my father or keep going on about it. There's an unjust shame that attaches to rejection that can be hard to shake off entirely. But they want to know, because they want to know who I am and who I was when I came to Corfu the month after I saw my father. I can't imagine this will be the last time they ask about it. Moments like that day with my father catch the light more often than you expect or want: in stories, questions; in the reflection of our eyes in the window of a minibus. But the boys' sympathetic interest, their innate sense of its relevance, makes me feel that I can share just about anything with them.

'I know it's hard to understand,' I say. 'But he couldn't really give me what I'd hoped for. It was all still a secret. *I* was still a secret. The truth didn't come out until much later, and by then it was too late for me to have a proper relationship with him, even if he'd wanted one. I pretty much gave up on him that month when he said *no thanks, can't do it.*'

'So, you just left Iceland and that was it,' Finnur says.

'That's how it had to be, I'm afraid. But look where I was heading,' I reply, at this instant thinking as much of him and Magnús as I am thinking about Corfu and the bays of shelter and even reclamation that it was about to offer.

5

New shoes

It was improbable that there would be work. Even the Pirate himself seemed unreal and dream-like now that a night had passed since we disembarked the ferry. Maybe there would be an altogether different person at the taverna this time – the real taverna owner. But when we got there the following morning, the doors were already wide open, and the Pirate was awake and seemingly at work himself. He was seated at his table near the kitchen, with his white phone, an ashtray and a can of Coke as his only companions.

He waved us in and offered us cigarettes. I hadn't had breakfast, and I didn't like smoking on an empty stomach, but then an old woman, who was helping in the kitchen, stepped out and offered us coffee, and I took one of the Pirate's cigarettes for later. She was so small she was hidden entirely by the bench when she went back into the kitchen, except for the occasional flash of a white bandana that she wore across her tied-back white-grey hair.

'My mother,' the Pirate said.

'Hello,' I called to her, and saw her hand wave over the counter.

'*Kalimera*,' she said.

The Pirate was dressed in the same blue shirt that we'd seen him in the day before, now traced with what looked like large amounts of cooking oil. He seemed irritated by the world and its demands, just as on the day before. His mother returned with black coffee and small glasses of water for me and Paul. As she put them down, I noticed thick, bent fingers, which seemed too large for the rest of her body and made it difficult for her to hold the tiny coffee cup. 'There you are,' she said in a thick Greek accent, and rested her hand on my shoulder and then on my head.

'Thank you,' I said.

The Pirate's mum stood beside me for a moment until I picked up the cup, as if to make sure that I was going to drink it, and then she took her hand away and left for the kitchen. She began washing plates and pots from the night before. I sipped the coffee: it was syrupy but dry, and extremely strong. I'd never tasted anything quite like it.

'Good?' asked the Pirate.

'Very good. I hope I'm early enough,' I replied.

'Yes, yes. Coffee first. Then, work.' He added to Paul that he didn't have any jobs for him today, but probably tomorrow. I was glad Paul had made the effort to come up with me, though, to remind the Pirate there were two of us searching for work. We'd need more than one income if we were ever going to save enough money to get back to Glasgow.

We sat in silence and smoked. Now and then, the Pirate coughed and sniffed and drank some of his Coke. Neither Paul nor I knew what to say. Around us, the taverna was as wearied as the Pirate – by time and grease and late nights. But it was lovely in its cluttered joinery of bottles and souvenirs. One part of the back wall was lined with pictures of the Pirate with dinner guests, all in the same pose of toasting, arm in arm, with small glasses of red wine. The tables near the front windows were still covered in chequered tablecloths from the night before, as well as morsels of lamb and chicken. I had the feeling I was the only one who noticed them.

We waited and waited, until eventually the white phone rang, and the Pirate spoke to someone on the other end in Greek. When he hung up, he opened his posture and did his best to smile. 'They are ready,' he said.

He stood up and gestured for me to come to the front door with him. 'Walk that way until you get to the fork. Go right and up the hill a few steps. There is a lady waiting for you. She is the shoe seller. *Cobbler.*' He giggled, seemingly at the sound of the word, and said it again. 'You are going to work for her. They asked me to send a polite boy. Are you a polite boy?'

'A sweetie pie,' Paul said on my behalf.

'Don't worry. They will tell you what to do. It's easy.' He turned to me and glanced at my clothes. 'You are a fucking mess, but the ladies will like your hair. But you are a polite boy, right?'

'I hope so,' I said.

The Pirate nodded. 'It isn't far. Stay on the right. Look for a lady on her own outside a house.' He smiled. 'Go. The lady is waiting.'

Two women, not one – a middle-aged woman and a younger lady – stood waiting for me in the street. They were the same height and wore the same hard, high-waisted skirts with their shirts tucked in neat. I said hello, and the older of the two women

53

shook my hand. 'This is my daughter,' she said. Then, 'No English.'

She pointed to a lower section of outside wall, a bucket of lime, and a broad brush that sat beside it. 'Two thousand drachmas,' said the daughter with a fair English accent. Remembering that manners were a part of the job, and that it might not be obvious how finely mannered I was, I agreed on the price, and nodded to show that I understood what to do. To be sure they knew what I knew, I mimed lime-washing the lower wall. The daughter smiled and said, 'Coffee first.'

'Yes. Coffee first,' said the mother.

Their house was tucked demurely into a street corner, an inside elbow of the main road as it climbed. The shoe sellers led the way up a narrow stone staircase that divided the house from a neighbour's grounds, which had a more definite presence. Then they invited me into a small, cool living room with a view of the street.

We sat in a triangle of wooden seats. The two women faced me but didn't speak. I was very mindful of the Pirate's instructions and how I'd been sent here as a representative of polite behaviour, even polite *male* behaviour, and I knew this usually meant more than mere silence. And yet, I also sensed that the main obligation now was to wait for an appropriate amount of time to pass before the mother made the coffee. To be patient and decorous.

So, we waited.

At last, she stood up and left the room, and the daughter fetched a low coffee table to place between us. Then the mother came back, without coffee. While the coffee brewed, we remained fixed in our narrow triangle of politeness.

I smiled, and the daughter smiled, and we waited.

'My mother owns the shoe shop,' said the daughter.

'Yes, the Pirate said that.'

The two women looked at my shoes and then at each other.

'You have seen it?' asked the daughter.

'Yes, when we arrived in town yesterday. The Pirate is helping us.'

'Your shoes are very bad,' said the daughter.

'Yes,' I answered.

'Very broken,' she went on.

The truth of the matter was that they were getting worse than that. There were holes at the end of my big toes. Wide rips lapped along the in-steps. The soles were beginning to go floppy.

'Maybe I should start on the wall?' I asked.

'No,' said the daughter. She spoke to her mother in Greek. 'What size are you?'

'Fourteen,' I replied. 'I mean, forty-eight.'

The daughter sighed. 'Please wait here,' she said.

I was left in the living room on my own while the shoe sellers walked out of the room. I heard their voices in the street as they passed the front window. I wondered about them, about why there wasn't a husband for either of them. And why they insisted on polite labourers when they had to get help. They were so trusting to leave me on my own in their living room, with all their family ornaments and keepsakes out on counters and the table.

After a few minutes, they returned. The daughter held a pair of football boots with fixed studs. 'You try these,' she said.

'Oh,' I said, 'football boots.' But I was to try them on immediately. 'I think they're too small,' I said, as I squeezed into them. Mercifully, they were a size nine, and couldn't possibly fit my feet. 'Thank you for looking for me.'

With relief, I began to put my old shoes on again. The mother uttered instructions as her daughter left again.

'You like Corfu?' asked the mother.

'Very much,' I answered.

'Not too hot now,' she said.

'It's perfect weather, isn't it,' I agreed. 'Just right.'

'This is better,' said the daughter, returning with shiny black boots. They were beautiful, steel-capped and watertight, but still much too small – size eleven at best.

'Thank you very much,' I said, leaving my shoes on. 'But I can't accept these.'

'Your shoes are bad,' said the mother.

I put on the boots, and in the first steps felt already the dreaded pinch of new, ill-fitting shoes that will never give. Remembering my manners, I decided I'd bear it until I could change back.

'Go to work now,' said the daughter.

'Happy?' asked the mother.

'Very happy,' I replied, and went off to lime.

As I reached for my old shoes, the mother said, 'No, no. No good. Rubbish!'

A moment later, I heard my shoes thrown into the outside bin. They were comfortable shoes, and I have to admit that at that moment I didn't much care if they seemed shabby. But the women felt there was no choice, and there was nothing I could do but to wear my new boots for the rest of the workday. I felt deeply grateful and in immense pain at the same time.

I couldn't remember ever having received such unbidden and unexpected generosity from complete strangers. It was a touching gesture: to offer shoes to a person working for you, even if they were in your service for just one day. I absorbed their hospitality and kindness, and something else as well – another ethical imperative that was at play and that centred on responsibility and community. I suppose it was the very warm sensation of being welcomed, and the signal of almost family-like acceptance that came with it.

It took until late afternoon to finish liming; the women kept stopping me to feed me and give me more coffee, each time making me come up to their lounge room and sit with them as I drank or ate. My heart rate went up with each sip of coffee. The conversations between us didn't expand beyond weather and the loveliness of Corfu and the village of Karousades, but the atmosphere eased, and I stopped feeling like I ought to say something to prove my manners.

It was enjoyable work, too: the lime wash was silty and stuck well to the rough walls. When I was finished, the shoe seller's daughter gave me two thousand drachmas, as promised, and said she hoped it was enough for a day's work. It was less than twenty dollars, but all that really mattered was to be earning again.

I said goodbye and walked down the hill towards the Pirate's taverna. My feet were in agony, so I walked as slowly as I could. The village was busy now. People shopping at the butcher's, picking up odds and ends at the grocer's at the fork in the road. There was a lot of waving between drivers, and between drivers and their friends sitting together on stools against the front of houses. Yelling-talking, too – or so it seemed to me. Friendly but extremely loud.

The taverna was also loud and crowded, with men drinking coffee and ouzo; there were no female customers. They were served by a tall, wiry man wearing a blue apron whom I hadn't seen that morning. The Pirate was in the same spot at his corner table, sitting on his own. But he was drinking red wine and talking over the music and across the tables.

He waved when he saw me. 'Come in!' he called, standing to greet me.

I noticed a first glaze of drunkenness in his eyes. He smiled and directed me towards a table next to his – not his own, which he seemed to want for himself alone. He called out to the tall man to bring bread and wine, and soon the man emerged with a large bottle and a very small glass that he filled to the brim. I took a sip and toasted the Pirate.

'My wine,' he said proudly.

'Delicious,' I said. It tasted like rosé, although less fragrant and more refreshing.

'Did it go okay?' he asked.

I had the sense from the Pirate's upbeat manner that he already knew the answer to his question, and that the women had called ahead. I pointed at my new shoes. 'Yes. They gave me these.'

The Pirate leant across to look and began to giggle. He spoke in Greek to the men around us and got up and patted me on my back and then on my face. Apparently, I'd achieved something worthwhile, but I felt embarrassed by the attention and by whatever it was they were saying. I mumbled that the women had given me the shoes because they didn't like the state of my old ones.

'I knew it would go well,' he said. And then for a second time he giggled.

Never mind, I thought. Regardless of whatever it was that amused the Pirate, I'd finished a day's work without complaints from his customers and we had twenty dollars and I had new shoes, even if they didn't fit.

At the Pirate's insistence, I had a second glass of wine and then I said I should go the campsite. I wanted to tell Paul that it had gone well. I took the money out of my pocket. 'Do I pay you something?' I asked.

'No! That is your money,' he exclaimed. 'You want more work?'

I wondered to myself what was in it for him.

'I will help you,' he said. 'You come here, only to me, and you always have work.' He lit a cigarette and watched the red tip. 'Here,' he said, standing again and leading me across the room. 'Andreas!'

A man in his forties turned his face to me and shook my hand. There was another rapid exchange in Greek, much gesticulating and nodding and then a resolution, a contract formed: one to which I was a mute, unknowing spectator while also being, it seemed, its main subject matter.

At its close, Andreas said he had labouring work for three of us.

'I will take you and your friend, and also Felix. If you are good workers, then three weeks' work.' Andreas held up three fingers to confirm. Three boys, three weeks. 'Wait here at the bench at six. If you're late,' he said, 'I have to leave without you.'

'See!' said the Pirate as he let me go. 'Everything is great now!'

As most surely it was.

6

Our perceptions of danger

Corfu, September 2022

What would I, as a parent of two teenage boys, offer as advice to the boy-man of eighteen who had just completed a day's liming and was about to befriend a pirate? Perhaps something along the lines of: *Glad today went well. Why not have a couple more days in Corfu. I'll send some money so you can leave after that.*

What would Finnur reply? *Calm down, Dad, it's fine!*

And, of course, he would be right. Why on earth would you want to curtail the experiences that were unfolding for me in 1990? I loved the island, we were being taken in by the villagers, there was work and, yes, even the hint of a possible love interest. I was given the time and place to rediscover how much there was to experience in life, even after a loss of the kind I'd experienced in Iceland. I hesitate to call it a rescue; the word looks too melodramatic on the page. But that's how it was.

Why would you leave? Certainly not yet.

The boys firmly agree. 'I can see why you wanted to stay,' says Magnús, though his reasons are a little different from mine. 'If you'd left as soon as you had enough money to go, you

61

wouldn't have got to know the village or anyone. Not properly.'

'Are you glad you're here? Does it feel at all odd that I've asked you to come and see it?'

'Nah. I'm glad. Being here makes it real.'

'I think so, too. Being in the setting of a story changes it.' Not only making it feel more real, but also more personal to the listener or reader. They can begin to add their own narrative to the one they're hearing. It's what I would like the boys to do: steal some of this for themselves, as pirates might do.

Around mid-morning, we pile back into the scratched hatchback for brunch at a bakery in the nearby town of Acharavi. I've had breakfast there a few times during the last week before Olanda and the boys arrived, since I picked up the rental car and could get around more easily. They serve good espresso and all kinds of rolls, croissants and sweets, and it's popular with both tourists and locals; I especially like it because of a corner table on the front balcony that's monopolised by half-a-dozen old men arguing, or seeming to argue, about the goings-on in the newspapers they bring with them. They add dignity and age to the main street that's mainly given over to minimarkets, bars and tourist shops.

Olanda orders for us all, while the boys and I find a table. When she joins us, we watch with the boys as helmetless scooter riders race between cars going in all kinds of directions. We decide the driving here is how people walk on a busy pavement: there's weaving and last-minute swerving, with the addition of speed and drivers' exclamations about the extraordinary stupidity of all other drivers. Yet the locals seem to step from their cars and these abrasive encounters transformed, walking idly towards whatever task is at hand, smoking, speaking genially on the phone, waving to friends — the momentous anger of minutes before forgotten.

The boys tend to make fun of my careful driving and nervousness about their safety. In part, it's because I am by nature a calm person. I also like trying new things, taking risks – in fact, I've never paid much attention to my own safety. But even they are shocked by the traffic here. 'How come there aren't there more accidents?' Magnús asks. 'People are literally driving straight at each other until the last second.'

'Like in a rugby game,' Finnur adds.

'Or basketball,' says Magnús.

Much beeping, too. At first, I thought it must be impatience. But that is just one of the many usages of the beep that I have observed and noted over the past weeks. I announce my theory of the beeps while the boys finish their breakfasts.

Beep Type 1: Hello, my friend (sometimes a short double-beep).

Beep Type 2: (Stopping next to a café/shop) I'd like that order I rang about.

Beep Type 3: I'm here, watch out.

Beep Type 4: I'm here even though it's a one-way street in the other direction, so watch out.

Beep Type 5: You shouldn't be in this one-way street, and I'd like you to move back.

Beep Type 6: You have every right to be making that turn/slowing down/observing road rules, but I don't like it because it is delaying me (with yelling).

Beep Type 7: Why are you such a bad driver? It confuses and pains me (hand on forehead). You're going to kill us both.

Beep Type 8: Leave this village, you're a disgrace. Go on. Leave.

'I'm glad you're doing the driving,' Olanda says when I finish. 'Is there a beep for that?'

'I wouldn't mind trying it,' Finnur says. 'I *think*.'

He got his learner's permit just a couple of months ago and has had his first few drives up and down a quiet street near our place, and in the local church car park. After he had his first proper lesson, Finnur recounted how the instructor noticed that he was a bit nervous and asked him whether there was anyone in the family who didn't like cars and roads. 'I said my dad likes cars,' he told us, loyally, 'but I also said you get pretty nervous about me driving.' The instructor assured him that it was usually a good thing: once Finnur had his confidence, his carefulness would make him a better driver.

'I'm getting more relaxed, aren't I?' I ask. 'Fussing over you less?'

Finnur isn't sure. 'I would say you still worry more than you need to. I mean, it's nice. You care.' He pauses. 'You care a *lot*.' He considers it some more. 'But yeah, you do seem to be getting more chill these days.'

When an accident of the kind I had always feared did befall the block where we live, it wasn't one of our sons who was hurt, but a neighbour's eight-year-old boy. It happened during that quiet part of a Saturday afternoon when everyone was pottering around. The boy next door was scootering in front of his garage while his father was washing the car. This was on a slope that ran down from the garage to the main driveway; the boy lost control of his scooter just as a car came along. He slipped and slid underneath the car, from the side, not the front.

The driver, another of our neighbours, wasn't speeding or doing anything hazardous. It was just a terrible piece of bad luck. She stopped straight away, and the poor boy was trapped underneath, screaming as he was burnt by the underside of the vehicle.

When we heard his cries, Olanda and I ran outside and tried to help. The driver was in shock and didn't know what to do next. She stood behind the vehicle with her hands pressed to her mouth. The parents were beside themselves but didn't know what to do. We turned the car engine off and looked underneath to see the boy with his legs folded up against the muffler. By then, though I would say less than a minute had passed, lots of other people had come out of their houses. As a group, we made the decision to lift the car and try to slide the boy out. The boy's mother was imploring us to hurry. With some six people on one side, we raised the side of the car for long enough for her to be able to pull him free and comfort him in the shade while we waited for an ambulance to arrive.

It was at that point, with the immediate emergency over, that I glanced up at our balcony and saw that Finnur and Magnús were watching; had been watching the whole time. I ran upstairs and spoke to them. They were scared for their friend, the boy who lived next door and whom they knew from school, and they were proud of us and the others in the block who'd got him free.

The sound of the boy's screams stayed with us all for many nights after, and for a while we all had trouble sleeping.

The accident made me more vigilant about people speeding in the driveway. But what I also noticed was that it *didn't* seem to make me any more or less nervous about the hazards in the boys' lives. That is, the reality of the incident and my witnessing of it didn't alter my perceptions of the dangers. I realised then that events like this lay outside my fears, and that my concerns weren't necessarily proportional to what was happening; they expressed something in me as a father. An intense desire for their safety.

The question that I asked myself – what can I do to keep my children safe? – was one I shared with all the parents I knew. But my answers were so protective. Or maybe overly *present* was the right term for it. Was I supplanting my father's absence in my life with a heightened presence of my own? Or was I merely indulging my fears as a parent?

And how might I change that, I wondered, and allow the boys the freedoms I liked in my life, and had enjoyed as a child and a young man? Some people argued that my generation of parents was too protective, too involved. We didn't know how to let go, stand back.

I'd only recently turned seventeen when I left for my gap year, with a thousand dollars in my pocket and no plans besides getting work as soon as I could. And I was only eighteen when we found ourselves joining the world of the Pirate. There was a safety net: a return plane ticket to Brisbane and a credit card that Mum had said I could use in an emergency. But she'd let me go. A brave act, I realised now.

One of my doctoral students in creative writing, Fiona, works as an emergency physician at the Queensland Children's Hospital. We are a similar age. Over the years, I've seen her at the hospital if the boys have hurt themselves playing sport. At the end of our supervision meetings, I sometimes ask for her advice about their development, or about parenting.

When I told her about the accident in our block, she said she knew about it already: the story of a group of neighbours lifting a car to get a child out had travelled through the hospital.

'That was at your place?' she asked.

We talked about the accident, and then I asked her about my nervousness about the boys getting hurt, and what I saw as my over-worrying. 'Anxiety like this depends on a lot of factors,' she said. 'Often, it's because of the upbringing the parents have had.'

'But my childhood was so free,' I said. 'It was just me and Mum, and growing up in Iceland in those days was so different, really very open; we didn't have be in at any particular time. No-one kept an eye on us. And I worked from around the age of eight, without supervision. People used to say that Mum was strict because she made me come home by midnight. They just wanted their kids outside – in summer, I mean. It feels unfair to my boys that I fuss over them the way I do.'

Fiona explained that these things play out unpredictably, sometimes in inverse relation to our past or the actual nature of the threat. Broadly speaking, our generation seemed very motivated to provide safety, whereas our parents had been less concerned about it. It could be difficult to see the reality of the threats in front of us. 'Let me give you an example,' she went on. 'What do you think is the one object that I and, I know, quite a lot of other staff at the emergency ward would love to see taken out of homes where there are small children living?'

I gave it some thought. 'I would guess fires – fireplaces, stoves, that kind of thing. Knives, maybe.'

Fiona smiled and shook her head. 'Coffee tables.'

I touched my left eyebrow and an old scar that is partly concealed by it. 'Coffee table,' I said. 'I think I was about two.'

'There, you see,' said Fiona.

'Oh god, now I'm going to be getting rid of all the coffee tables in our place,' I joked.

*

67

After brunch, we walk from the Acharavi main street down to the pebble beach that lies a few hundred metres away. The boys take off their shirts and run into the water, which has more waves than is usual on Corfu, but it's nothing like the surf we get at home. I watch them standing in the water side by side, with just their shoulders and heads showing, and wonder what they're talking about. Something tells me it's their own footnote to the conversation we had about my father. I wonder what they see as the effects of my unusual upbringing, fatherless and rather free. Effects on me, and by turns on them, as well.

As I watch them, I recall something Mum has mentioned to me: that she'd known an Englishman who wanted to settle down with her and adopt me. He said that there would have to be more discipline, though – that he could tell I had my own way a bit too much. It was true that in Iceland we children did more or less what we liked, and I know from having worked there as a high school teacher that things haven't changed much. The schools are forever pleading with parents to make their children sleep more, so that they don't fall asleep in class.

But it was my verbosity that people noticed most about me, and how Mum was happy to let me speak as though I were an adult at the table, with an equal part to play. She'd noticed that, as long as I could be involved, I seldom complained. I knew everyone at her office by name, and would spend hours chatting to them. One of my favourite places in the world was a basement room filled with drawer after drawer of small machine parts, replacements for the tools that the business imported. The old man who worked down there had an encyclopaedic knowledge of them, and would humour me as I asked him about each and every one. He put the parts on a workshop bench, one by one, and explained them to me.

He was like Mum in that respect: accepting of children's points of view, and their right to know things.

Growing up in England and Australia, Mum had had a very strict mother who felt children should know their place. Her mother believed in the old expression 'spare the rod and spoil the child'. So, when Mum heard that the Englishman's involvement in disciplining me was a condition of the relationship, she decided against it. 'I wasn't going to be told how to discipline my son,' she told me. 'That was for me to decide. Not some man. Who did he think he was?'

Maybe he thought discipline was a sign of commitment or diligence as a parent, but it isn't how Mum expressed her love, and at least discipline hasn't been over-present in our family, either. I don't wish to punish or constantly constrain the boys or always be telling them how to behave. That is not how my protectiveness manifests. Most of the time, they get things right without me – especially when left to do so. Or get away with it when they don't.

There, I think. *They do manage, don't they.*

A ball being tossed around by another family lands between the boys, and Magnús reaches forward and throws it back. I'm sorry to see that it puts an end to their chat, and they start to wade back in. They slump down onto the towels with a sigh and seem to sink into the ground with the weight of complete relaxation and ease.

My own thoughts linger on the sight of them in the water, talking. I feel a sweetly melancholy pride in seeing them confide in each other, without my involvement. For it's a kind of independence, and a guarantee or promissory note that tells me they'll look out for each other. Listen to what they each have to say.

'Listen,' I murmur into my beach towel, as Mum listened to me. Allowed a voice and an involvement that was surely part of why I'd ended up in Corfu with Paul, falling into the companionship of a pirate.

7

Islands of our own

Corfu, September 1990

Two weeks before we arrived in Corfu, while Paul and I were still making our way through Europe, we celebrated my eighteenth birthday in Munich, at the beer festival. To begin with, we sat shyly at the end of one of the long wooden benches, unsure even of how to order. But then a group at the other end of the bench told us to join them. They were older and wanted to feed us and pay for our beers. It must have been because we didn't know what we were doing.

That night, we slept at the train station. If you got in before the doors shut, the police and security guards let you find a spot in the hall. We nestled up against a tiled wall, and Paul fell asleep straight away, his head on my shoulder, his snores reaching towards the cathedral-like roof. Very early the next day, a security guard tapped our toes and said it was time to go, find some breakfast. It wasn't exactly a hospitable way for dealing with young drunks, but it worked. The city had a system to protect us – from ourselves as well as from those who might want to harm the young.

Maybe that was what the Pirate was like, too. He wasn't

especially pleasant, but he offered his own way of taking people in and looking after them. After our conversation at the taverna, I rushed back to the campground, my chest filled with joy and relief. We'd been promised three weeks' work! It was too good to be true. Paul jumped in celebration when I told him, Felix staring at us as though we were a little mad. I left Paul to tell Helena and offer her some of the money I'd earned that day. She waved it away. 'Keep that for now,' she said. 'Pay me after you've done a few days. You might even be able to afford a tent each.'

That night, most of us at the campsite had dinner together by the fire. Bella and Joe had been to Kalami, which they told me was well known because the Durrell family had lived there in the 1930s. Michelle said she wanted to go there, too, because she'd read the books Gerald Durrell and his brother Lawrence had written about the island. I'd heard about them from Mum, but that was as much as I knew.

'Those wonderful books are why we included Corfu in our itinerary,' said Bella. 'You'll have to read them. You'll *have* to.'

We all promised we would when we got the chance. As it turned out, not only did I read the Durrells at university, but I also went back to those books again and again, each time enraptured by the stories the brothers told and their very different ways of telling them.

Felix was sitting on the ground with his paper plate on his crossed legs. A bit of sauce squirted out from his roll onto his leg. He scooped it up with the tip of his index finger, looked at it and smiled, and licked his finger clean. When he saw me watching, he laughed and said, 'Saucy!'

There was something about him that didn't quite add up: he was meant to be on leave from the army, but apart from his physique, which was muscular and lean, he seemed completely untouched by military life, as though he'd been in Greece for years. It made me more and more curious about him, and whatever it was he was concealing.

Michelle had finished her dinner and sat with her guitar by her side. I had the feeling she was waiting for someone to suggest that she play a song, but so far no-one had voiced the idea. 'You didn't manage to leave Corfu again today?' I asked her.

'No. But I have to go back to my course soon. It's already started. If I don't go back in a couple of weeks, I lose my spot. There's probably a very serious letter from the university waiting for me at home. I bet I'm in trouble.'

'Not as much as me,' said Felix to himself.

'You don't want to go back to Geneva?' I asked Michelle.

'Oh, Geneva is very …' she searched for the word, 'proper. Everyone does what they're supposed to do.'

'Except you,' I said. 'You're going to be late for the beginning of semester.'

'Did you like your day in the village?' she asked. 'Did you work hard?'

'I liked it very much. I lime-washed a wall for the first time in my life and I was given a pair of shoes.' I had taken them off and couldn't show Michelle, but she smiled at the thought of it.

'Greek people are the most generous people in the world,' she said. 'Sometimes, they get upset if they can't give you something. If you go into their house, they show you around as if you just have to ask for something and it's yours. I love them so much.'

'Scots are like that, too,' I said. 'Paul and all the other people I met there. To be honest, I didn't know what to do this morning when the women insisted I take the shoes. I thought I should probably say no, because it was too generous, but that would have been rude.'

'They would have hated it if you said no.'

'They don't actually fit.'

'They might stretch,' Michelle said. 'Have you been around the village? It's very historical. Do you like historical places?'

It was a rather sudden turn in the conversation, but I came to learn it was how she liked to converse, in sharp turns, like a slalom skier. 'It was one of my favourite subjects at school,' I said. 'I was good at history and English.'

'Me, too. I like stories more than my course. I go looking for them. Old stories, especially. When I arrived, I made a guess that the name Karousades was from *carousel*; you know, a fairground ride. Or maybe *carouse*. That means to drink a lot. Did you know that?'

'Not really. I thought *carouse* meant amorous.'

'It can mean that as well, yes. You're English, so you know better. But anyway, I was speaking to a lady at the church, and she told me that Karousades is named after a lost city called Karousa, on the Black Sea, because the village was founded by refugees from Karousa when their city was destroyed.'

'A village of exiles,' I said.

'That's it,' she said. 'But here's another bit of this story. I think you will like this. The lady said not to listen to anyone who says the village is named after *krasades*.'

'What's so bad about that?'

'It means *wine*! I don't think she liked the idea that she might live in a place called *Wine*.' Michelle laughed to herself and picked up her guitar and looked down at the frets.

I liked her a lot: how her mind seemed to dart between subjects, her eyes moving quickly, too, as though she was having trouble keeping up with herself.

'Time to play, I think,' she said. 'You can stay and drink and listen. If you go to bed early again, I'll think you don't like my music.'

Her playing improved now that she wasn't trying to master 'Take On Me'. I was in the mood to celebrate my day, and I stayed on as more and more people arrived from their island explorations and sat by the fire, dinnertime steadily being nursed into a party. Later, Michelle passed the guitar to me, and I strummed the few chords I knew, and she hummed along.

Paul spent most of the night talking to Felix. When we went back to the tent at midnight, he said Felix was great fun but that he was a mad fucker underneath it all. 'I've known plenty of crazy guys like him,' he said. 'They either laugh or lose it, but that's all they have. No gears in between.'

'Maybe we should keep a bit clear of him, then,' I suggested.

'Don't be stupid, Kári,' Paul said. 'You don't keep clear of people just because they're a bit suspect. Where would that leave us in life?'

'True,' I said, thinking of the Pirate as well. Paul, even. And, in fact, I wasn't being suspicious or cynical towards Felix. That wasn't how I ever felt about the people I met, even when they didn't quite make sense to me. I preferred to try to figure them out. But I didn't want to jeopardise what we'd found in Corfu; it was already something I was trying to hold on to just the way it was, as though it was already a place of return.

*

The next day, we only just made it to the taverna at six, but we got there. No-one had an alarm clock or a watch, but Helena came to our tents at five-thirty, before she went to meet the morning ferry arriving from Brindisi, and checked if we were up. We had to run up the hill; when we reached the village, we sat puffed on the bus-stop bench outside the taverna and waited. The Pirate wasn't awake yet, and it was perfectly still in the village. The bright colours of the houses were paled, like flowers in winter.

Felix looked at my boots. 'Do they hurt?' he asked. 'You run funny.'

'They're too small,' I said.

He pointed at his broad, sun-tanned feet. 'I only wear scandals,' he said.

'Sandals,' I said.

'Hmm?'

'*Sandals.* A scandal is something else.'

'Even when we are working,' he continued, merrily. 'I am never wearing the boots again!'

'Won't the army make you wear them when you go back?'

'You can't wear scandals in the army,' Paul joked.

Before Felix could respond, or we could make another comment at Felix's expense, Andreas's van pulled up in front of us. He told us to jump onto the tray at the back. We clambered on and he drove back down the hill, passed the campsite and went on. It was very cold, but there was a white mist on the hills that promised it would get hot later. I had no idea where we were going, but I didn't mind. It felt good to be busy, knowing we'd work all day and then come back to the same place that night. A day with shape, a circle, like the ones we make years later when we come back again.

The van climbed further into the hills. To begin with, they seemed a distant elevation of woods and olive trees that barely emerged from the haze. But as we got higher, carved ridges came into shape, each one topped with a village of terraces and tight, winding lanes, just like Karousades, the hillside homes eventually yellowing as the sun climbed with us and hit their fronts. This early, the only people up were the old, ambling between morning tasks, sweeping just as much as we'd seen two days before, when we'd first arrived. Felix called out good morning to them in Greek and then he began singing in German, songs like the ones we'd heard in Munich, and that he knew from the army.

'C'mon. Let's sing!' he yelled. 'It's better than sitting here feeling cold.' Paul and I weren't sure the villagers wanted to wake up to us singing Austrian army songs, but we made a muted attempt at joining in. 'There!' cried Felix, heroically. 'Now we are feeling better, aren't we!'

I didn't have a map of the island, or even a clear mental picture of it as a whole, and all I ever learnt about the location of Andreas's building site was that it was half an hour's drive from Karousades and sat on the side of one of these mountain villages, within sight of the coastline. The project consisted of a block of villas that was being raised at one end of his farm. When we arrived, he said that our job for the day, and the next few days if we worked hard, was to take mixed concrete from the side of the farmhouse, near the farm gates, to where it was needed on site.

The concrete mixer was already running. Felix began shovelling in mix and sand and pebbles, while Paul and I pushed wheelbarrow-loads along wooden planks that lay between the mixer and the brick-and-steel-rod shells of the new villas. After an hour, my back and the tops of my legs began to burn. I couldn't draw in my arms when I put the wheelbarrow down, and I slowed my pace. Paul also seemed distressed.

When Felix saw us struggle to keep up, his temper began to fray. 'You aren't going fast enough,' he yelled. 'You have to keep up with the mixer.' If we didn't do that, the mix wouldn't be as good, and Andreas wouldn't have us back. 'Faster! Faster!' he said. 'Move the fucking borrow, you idiots!'

'Barrow,' Paul said.

'Whatever the fuck it's called,' Felix said.

We began to rush, and with that both of us spilt a full load of cement each, off the side of the planks and into the mud by their side. Andreas smiled and said not to worry about it, but I could tell that you didn't get many spilt loads before you weren't asked back. We scooped up the wasted cement and dumped some of it in the skip, Felix ready to explode with frustration.

'Did no-one ever teach you how to steer?' he yelled.

At nine, we stopped for coffee. When I sat down, I didn't think I'd be able to get up. Felix noticed my grimace and said, 'You need ten minutes' rest. In a few days, you will get fitter and stronger and then you won't even notice the pain.' He said it matter-of-factly; I felt like I was being inducted into an Austrian health regime that he'd been part of for years. But he wasn't patronising, even though he didn't seem to have any discomfort himself, not a bit. 'Have you worked here for long?' I asked.

'Two months. Since I left the army.'

'Oh? I thought you said you were on holidays.'

'Well, I say holidays. A *long* holiday.' He gave me a broad smile but didn't go on. There wasn't time to talk about it now; coffee break was over. 'You should take a turn on the mixer. It hurts in different places.' He said it like that was a good thing.

After pushing wheelbarrows of cement for two hours, shovelling into the mixer felt enjoyable. I even had pauses between loads, while Paul and Felix were pushing the barrowloads into the villas. Next, Paul had a turn at the mixer, and from then on we rotated the work. It dawned on me that Felix was taking a step down in status for us, from mixer to carrier. 'Thank you for this,' I said, when we were standing beside the mixer together.

'Pfft,' he said. 'What do I care what I do?'

I'd never worked on a building site, and so I had no idea of how the day would be broken up. The next thing that happened was a blissful surprise. At twelve-thirty, all work on the site stopped. Andreas asked us to rinse down the mixer and the barrows, clean ourselves, and join him at the farmhouse. 'My family is waiting to meet you,' he said.

We walked up to a white building at the top of a rise that overlooked the new buildings but was also slightly out of sight. 'We will still live in this house,' Andreas said, 'after the villas are finished. My grandfather built it. My siblings wouldn't let me sell it, even if I wanted to.'

Lunch was served in a wide side room with high doors that opened to a terrace. Andreas asked us to take seats at a long table. A few minutes later, his wife came out with wine and water. She said hello and told us that her name was Iris. Her blue summer dress touched the ground as she walked around the table, and she had the same calm manner as Andreas – unrushed and warm. I think we all fell slightly in love straight away. She brought out thick-sliced bread; on a second tray came cold meats, salad and feta wrapped in damp paper.

Their three children joined the table. They greeted us shyly and stared at each other with the look of children who'd just been told how to behave while there were guests at the house.

Andreas conversed with the others at the table about what had been happening on site during the morning, and in between sentences he translated what he could for us into English. I said I guessed he must have studied in England, judging from his southern English accent.

'No. We are just very clever on Corfu,' he joked. 'Did you know that the first modern Greek university was here? It was started by the English, I have to admit.' Then he said something in Greek that must have been very funny, because his wife and children laughed loudly. He apologised and said it would be hard to translate, but we three foreigners found ourselves laughing along, such was their geniality, their home a study in stability and steady good fortune. I hoped they'd be pleased enough with today's efforts to give us more work. 'Are you going to back to Australia?' Andreas asked. 'Isn't it like paradise to be living there?'

'Yes, everyone says so,' I agreed. 'I have a place at university for next year and up to January to use my plane ticket home.'

'So, you can stay in Corfu for a while longer,' he said. Addressing us all, he asked, 'Will you come back to work for me tomorrow?'

We nodded happily and finished our lunch, and the plates were put away. The wine was very light, but it did make me feel sleepy. Andreas said to take ten more minutes for a cigarette and coffee, if we wanted it. I'd already seen how, in the hospitality industry, it was customary to feed staff and make sure they felt looked after, in part because the wages were bad. But this lunch was different from that: we were not only being fed; it seemed to me that we were being asked in, just as when I was invited into the shoe sellers' lounge room and sat waiting for my shoes. Words like *welcoming* and *generous* seemed inadequate to describe it, for it was deeper than hospitality and good manners. It was a form of love for the world and for strangers.

After we finished our coffee, there was only one more hour of work before it was time to clean up the site. I realised that labouring work here was all about surviving until lunch. Just after two, Andreas paid us three thousand drachmas each for the day's work, about thirty dollars, and drove us back to the campsite and made us promise, once again, not to sleep in the next day. He said he'd see us outside the Pirate's taverna at six.

In the years since, I've wondered if I will ever again feel quite as healthy and strong as I did after I showered that afternoon, had scraped the dried cement off my hands, and put on a pair of *scandals* that Felix had spare and insisted that I borrow, missaying the word deliberately now. He said he couldn't watch me in those boots, which did loosen eventually, but not for some weeks yet. I ached all over but I didn't mind. I was looking forward to going back to work on Andreas's site the next day.

With the longer view that I have in telling this story now, I notice how the physical ache, which gave me a sense of closeness to my body and an awareness of the outdoor world, was at that moment exactly what I needed. Physicality brought the mind and the soul closer to the surface of the skin and allowed other troubles to rest. Disembarking had offered more than just work and a place to stay: it had given me a routine, and some rest that allowed me to begin digesting the events of the month before. Taking the chance of finding something had a remedy that was in-built, irrespective of the outcome: a gesture of trust in others.

I sat contentedly outside the tent and smoked while Paul took his turn in the shower. It was cool; the afternoon breeze smelt of seawater and dried fruits, but when it dropped you noticed the bass earthiness of the groves, as well as the more treble-clef scents that reminded me of nettles, mint, nectarines and lilies.

Michelle was tidying up around her tent. It seemed she'd adopted the local penchant for sweeping and was taking care to remove dust and sand from the entrance. After she had finished, she was settling down to read a book when she saw me watching her. I waved and she walked over and asked if I was going to eat dinner at the campsite.

'I think we're going up to the Pirate's taverna,' I said. 'We've got some money at last. We'd better spend it.'

'That's fine,' she said.

'Will you play guitar?'

'Maybe later. If you're lucky.'

'Join us for dinner, if you like?' I said.

'I feel like staying here.' She held up her book. It was *Emma* by Jane Austen, which I'd noticed at the reception bookshelf. 'I'm sure I'll see you when you get back,' she added.

'How's the book?' I asked. 'It's funny how they have so many nineteenth-century novels.' Alongside the Austen and Brontë, there were works by Flaubert, Dickens, Eliot, even Anthony Trollope. You could do a literature course.

'I like her. She's wrong about just about everything.' Michelle laughed. 'For some reason, that makes her more interesting to me.'

'I prefer those kinds of characters, too,' I said. 'The ones who are still working things out. Will Emma get there in the end?'

'Definitely,' said Michelle.

Paul and Felix and I left for the Pirate's taverna at eight. It was a very different restaurant from what I'd seen the afternoon before: crowded, the air filled with smoke from cigarettes and the grill; quite a few other foreigners were there, too. Plaintive Greek ballads boomed out of corner speakers, at the same time as football was on the TV, the sound of the game surging when the crowd celebrated and merging with the music.

The Pirate, too, was a changed man from whom we'd met in the daytime hours. He was up on his feet, moving lightly between tables, on his toes even, singing as he poured wine into customers' glasses. 'Yassas!' he called to us as we walked in. 'Good, good. Over here, near the window. Lads, you must be hungry. Time to eat! Drink!'

No food was served yet, but from the kitchen came an unbearably good smell of grilled lamb, chicken and vegetables, olive oil and pepper and lemon and parsley. The window was half open, letting the smells out and letting in the evening air, still fragrant with pollen but a little dank now as well, from the cooling bitumen and the open stormwater drains.

I was starving but there were no menus, nothing listed on blackboards. I asked Felix how we were meant to order. 'Don't worry,' he yelled over the music, laughing as usual. 'You don't have to do anything.'

The stereo got louder and louder. I didn't understand the words, but they seemed to abound with loss and regret, and periodically the Pirate became transfixed by them, in the grip of deep emotion. The Greek customers' expressions matched the sadness in his voice and his halted stance, as though really the whole world should have stopped at that moment; whenever a pause in conversation allowed it, or a song chorus demanded they join in, the room swelled with their tender complaints.

I noticed, again, that there were no local women in the taverna: this hadn't changed since the previous afternoon. The women who were here now were foreigners, in couples and small groups. The atmosphere, though not blokey, was starkly different from what we'd experienced at lunch with Andreas and Iris. It wasn't a pub or restaurant or bar, not business-like in that way. It was something more akin to a small carnival; surely the Pirate couldn't manage something this boisterous every night.

He brought out his lovely red wine – as dry and thin, almost watery, as the glasses I'd had the day before – in two-litre bottles to share. It wasn't strong, but it brought a flush to our cheeks. I was tired from the day's work, and the inside heat and noise made me feel a little heady, if it wasn't the wine. I hoped there would be food soon. The Pirate got busier in the kitchen and only came out when he needed to serve wine, and now bread and olive oil, as well. The chicken and lamb turned slowly on spits next to the kitchen window, within sight.

As it finally neared time to serve the main meal, the local men began to leave; they hadn't eaten and seemed to be going home for their dinner. Suddenly, it became a taverna for foreigners alone. The music blazed on. We watched the football and the jagged movements of the tall, thin man who helped in the kitchen. He stood hunched over the grill beside the Pirate's mum, who'd now appeared, wearing her high skirt and blue bandana. She seemed even smaller and older beside the thin man. Neither of them looked into the dining room or said much to the other. The talking seemed to fall entirely to the Pirate.

We finished our two litres of wine as the streetlamps added their orange glow to the coloured restaurant lights inside. More tourists arrived, more Germans and English, and also a French group: three men in their sixties who must've been hikers. It was a full room, raucous, joyous, and as hot as mid-summer.

Whenever new customers stepped in, the Pirate repeated a routine: he flung his arms open and called, '*Yassas!*' and then he took his guests by their arms or shoulders and led them to a table, *a special table for them*, he insisted, seemingly left vacant for all time until they'd arrived and claimed it as an ancestral right. He often laughed for no particular reason, a bit like Felix would, and said, 'You are welcome in my taverna!' The guests laughed as well, polite as people are when they're happy and on holiday and will sit where they're told. 'No menu, no menu,' he exclaimed when he saw them looking for one. 'No prices. You will be happy, I promise. Everyone is happy here!'

Yes, everyone was happy. I loved it, and I marvelled at how different the Pirate was now that he was in full swing, at work in a way I couldn't have imagined when he was sitting moodily beside his white phone, smoking heavily, drinking Coke, virtually invisible to the outside world. This was a man who could really play the part of a pirate. He *was* the Pirate now, as witnessed by all – singer, cook, host. The Pirate of Karousades, released from his earlier self and in complete control of the room.

One of the groups had noticed a naive drawing of a pirate that hung on the back wall of the taverna. It portrayed the complete pirate scenario, including features that the Pirate, our pirate, lacked: a Caribbean backdrop, an eye patch, puffy breeches, a peg leg and a sword, and a woman slung over his shoulder. 'That's me, that's me!' the Pirate exclaimed, when he noticed that the picture was getting his customers' attention.

'Where's the parrot?' someone yelled. 'You need a cheeky parrot.'

The Pirate found this hilarious and doubled over in laughter. 'Yes, yes! You are right. I will ask to add it,' he said. He giggled on. 'Where is the parrot?' he said to himself as he left for more wine.

He brought out bottle after bottle; it was as though it would never run dry, an endless fairy-tale wine to match his fairy-tale act. He laughed and sang and asked where people were from, and everywhere they mentioned, he'd been there. 'I was a sailor,' he told them. 'I have sailed the world many, many times! I am the Pirate, remember! I have seen it all!'

Cheers! Skal! Prost!

Though we were hardly his most important customers, his sense of hospitality was unending, and he didn't forget us. In between serving groups, he brought us the dinner he thought we should have. After the bread and olive oil came a Greek salad with all the ingredients very fresh, heavily seasoned and drenched in olive oil. Then, grilled chicken and lamb and thick-cut chips with the skin on. The meat was salty and tender and flavoured by the grill. It was exquisite food, and I was nervous he was going to charge us a fortune. There was still no end to the wine, either. Felix said not to worry but, as more was brought out, I told the Pirate we had to be careful with our money until we worked more days. He shook his head. 'I give you a discount,' he said. 'Relax. Do you have enough food?'

'Yes, plenty,' I said.

He scanned the table. 'More wine, then,' he concluded.

At the end of the night, he charged us twelve hundred drachmas, or twelve dollars, for the three of us, for everything we'd had: four dollars each. Even though it was 1990, and even though much of the produce was his own and cheaper for him than buying in, this was a fabulously generous price. 'Eat here every night, boys,' he said as we stumbled out. 'I am looking after you.'

It was the best meal of my life, up to then and since.

The fire was burning low when we got back to the campsite, but I sat down with the others who were still up. Michelle was playing guitar, plucking the strings but not singing. I was tipsy and I couldn't take my eyes off her. I thought about my lack of consistency, how I sometimes missed Jessica, the girl I'd broken up with in Scotland, and at other times felt the pain tail away behind me, like the waves that trailed behind the ferry when we'd come into Corfu. That was alright, wasn't it? I asked myself. No-one was perfectly consistent all the time, not even the characters of an Austen novel.

Michelle smiled and put the guitar down. 'How was dinner?' she asked.

'The food's so good,' I said. 'You should have come up with us.'

'I didn't like the Pirate very much when I met him.'

'Oh, you've eaten there?'

'Yes, once. Only once. I guess he wasn't that bad. I don't know. No, he was awful, actually. Not to me. Just in his way. There are better places to eat in Corfu.'

'Is he creepy?' I asked her, remembering how none of the local women were there.

She thought about it. 'No,' she said slowly. 'But don't you feel like there's something a bit icky about him?'

'There was a lot of grease on his shirt,' I joked. 'I'm not sure about the hygiene standards.'

Michelle laughed. 'I'll know what it is if you don't get up tomorrow.'

'I should go sleep,' I said, reminded of the early start ahead, Andreas coming to get us at six.

'Do you have to?' she asked.

'No,' I said, easily swayed by her attention, 'not really. What do we talk about, then? I know. University. What are you going to study?'

'Finance,' she answered, determinedly.

'I thought you might say something else, like literature or history. You're so interested in culture and the island.'

'I would like to study art history but that isn't the same thing as sitting here at a campfire dreaming about it. Anyway, you know how it is — my parents want me to be in business. Are your parents like that?'

'Not really,' I said. 'My mum thinks I should do what makes me happy. She's never had a job she really liked. So she wants that for me.'

'You're lucky, then. What about your father? Is he as relaxed about it?'

'I don't really know him. I visited him last month, but it didn't go very well. He has his own life, another family.' I felt myself blush at the sound of my voice, the shame in describing my situation out loud.

Michelle took a little longer to resume her questions, too. 'So, you will go back to Australia next?' she asked.

'I have to go back to London first. That's where I get my flight, in December or January. We need to work and save so that we can get back. Believe it or not, we only have what we earned today: three thousand drachmas each. We arrived with nothing.'

Her eyes widened. 'But I guess three thousand buys a lot here,' she said, 'if you can earn that every day. Do you know how much a beer is?' She held up her can of Amstel. 'Thirty drachmas.'

'Whoa,' I said. 'That's a hundred beers a day.'

'What?'

'On the beer index. If we earn three thousand a day.'

'You don't ever have to be sober again.'

'It's too good to be true,' I said, laughing. 'You know, the Pirate only charged us four hundred each for dinner. We can actually *save* money here.'

Michelle frowned. 'Oh, who cares about the Pirate. Don't let him decide what you're going to do. I could lend you some money if you really need it,' she said, as though it was no big deal, and that money flowed as endlessly as the Pirate's wine. 'That way you can go back whenever you want, and you don't have to work for him.'

It was sweet and kind that people wanted to take care of us, but we were fine now. We'd found work. I shook my head. 'That's a lovely offer, but how would I ever pay you back?' There was a pause. 'I should go to bed,' I said. 'We'll lose our jobs if we sleep in.'

'Go to bed, then,' she said, and then touched my arm. 'I will ask you more about your life and all other important matters tomorrow,' she added, with a note of light self-deprecation. 'This is just how we are in Geneva. We want everything clear from the start.'

The start of what? I wondered as I walked back to my tent, where I found Paul asleep, his body splayed diagonally across the entire floor. I rolled him onto his side and made sure he had enough covers, played dad to my friend, as though he'd come into my life to teach me how to take care of another person.

He was already feeling better, too, I had noticed at dinner – Corfu was his remedy as much as it was mine. And

Michelle's, I guessed, even if she didn't like the Pirate very much. She was well off. You could tell it from her leisurely confidence, her unhurried way of examining us and the island. But she was also the same: a captive. Happiness had made a prisoner of her.

The next morning, our second on the site, it was Andreas who was late getting to the pick-up spot outside the Pirate's taverna. As we sat on the bench, we saw three girls about our age waiting for a bus. Felix said they would be on their way to college, which was in Corfu Town.

'I think that's the first time I've seen girls our age,' I said.

'You better leave them alone,' warned Felix, 'otherwise.' He made a stabbing gesture. 'The knife comes out if we go near the girls. I've been warned, many times.'

'I bet *you* have,' said Paul.

I'd heard something similar in Aviemore when Paul and I had worked there – an old-fashioned rule that resort workers should stay away from the young women in the village. 'It's weird, isn't it,' I said. 'People so welcoming, but then they lock away their girls as though they're some kind of fragile possessions that need to be kept safe.'

'That's not the same,' said Paul.

'Why?'

Paul gestured behind us at the Pirate's taverna. 'Because to them, we look like the pirates in town,' he said. 'Do you blame them if they don't trust us?' He gave me a playful hug. 'I trust you, though, big man.'

He might have been right about other young men. But I was no pirate, surely. No marauding thief. 'I guess I have to remember how I look to them,' I conceded, though I also felt he might be wrong about the villagers. I was certain they had more sense than to lump us in with just any old drifters. The shoe sellers had recognised something better in me, hadn't they? A *gentleman*, even, I thought to myself and was much too self-conscious to say to the other two.

Andreas arrived before one of us made the mistake of saying hello to the girls, and they turned away. I had the feeling that they were curious about us, but their glances in our direction had been cautious and measured; probably, they'd heard a version of the warning from their parents, too.

Once again, we climbed into the hills, Felix singing to wake himself up. I had brought my camera, and Andreas drove pretty carefully, I now realised, and slowly enough for me to be able to take photos. I passed the camera around to Paul and Felix, and we took it in turns to pose, pulling our jumpers over our heads, pretending to be monkeys. We weren't a threat to the locals, but we were definitely idiots. I didn't realise it – how could I when everything was going so well? – but there was danger enough in that.

8

Crumbling walls

Corfu, September 2022

I cherish the pictures we took that morning on the back of
Andreas's van. When we get in from the beach, I show a couple of
them to the boys. I'm so pleased I have them, because they give me
the full shock of seeing myself as almost another person entirely.
Not a boy, exactly, for I'm making my own decisions, unguided
by anyone or anything except the road and whoever we met. But
so very unrecognisable from whom I see in the mirror today: in
looks, but most especially in a presence in the moment, utterly
unconcerned about whether it's safe to be racing through the hills
on the open tray of a van, hardly aware of what it would mean to
fall or crash or even brake too quickly. In one picture, my long
hair is all over the place, I'm laughing, one arm raised in the air. It
is pure and total celebration. Alive, moving through life, a set of
eyes facing the world, and perfectly, unbreakably unsafe. Where
does that go?

'You wouldn't let us do it,' says Magnús.

'Well, you are a bit younger,' I say.

Finnur joins in. 'Only a year and a bit. Maybe you need

some kind of therapy,' he says, jokingly. 'Hasn't some psychologist written a book on how to accept that your kids are going to do really stupid things, just like you did when you were young?'

'Dozens, I expect.'

Magnús senses a possible title. 'Dad, you could call your book, *Dumb Things to Do with Your Sons*.'

'That's funny. I'll make sure I credit you.'

'You're not that bad,' says Finnur. 'Some kids have parents who are *way* stricter. You're only medium protective.'

It's a generous thing for him to say, and of course we hear the stories of parents who *won't let their kids do anything*, or so the gossip claims. But *medium protective* isn't quite what I'm aiming for. The young man in the picture seems to be demanding better than that.

In the evening, I take the hint and look up terms for what I seem to be struggling with. I'm an academic, after all. Don't be lazy; do the research, I tell myself. I begin to browse online. There's a Jungian-derived approach that talks about *a teenager's developmental individuation* and another site offering tips on how to *survive* as a parent. But I don't want to 'survive' my children. Another online resource mentions the *paradox* that most parents will feel when they want to let go of and hold on to their children at the same time. I recall hearing of a *daisy shape* effect, or that from the earliest ages, even as toddlers, children move out and back in a daisy-flower pattern, with the leaf becoming larger as they get older, but the shape remaining the same. It suggests that you can trust that your children will keep returning to you. The process isn't one of loss, but rather a widening of their lives.

The diagnostic language puts me off, though, even if it's also scientific and useful, I'm sure. When I think about my own family, it appears as a collection of stories and memories, and places where the past comes to light. I see experiences and conversations. Specific moments. Is that why it's so difficult to start thinking with broad principles of parenting in mind? How do I respond, then, if my very present way of fathering also makes it harder for me to let go? I've become so used to being needed in a very direct, day-to-day sense, the way many fathers have in the past decades. My generation has been much more involved in hands-on parenting, and for me very happily so, but we are not so practised in what that means for us when our children grow up.

Over a glass of rosé, I recall to Olanda the opening lines of Halldór Laxness's book *The Fish Can Sing*, a story about an orphan who's raised in the Reykjavík of the early twentieth century by an elderly couple who adopt him. In characteristically ironic style, the author tells us that next to losing one parent, the best thing that can happen to a child is to lose them both. He doesn't say why, but I suppose the loss ensures that the child can become someone interesting, complete in themselves. And also, perhaps, can have a very full relationship with their grandparents, which is so often the case in Iceland.

Olanda laughs and says I don't have to kill us off in order to give the boys a sense of freedom.

'What do you suggest, instead?' I ask.

'I think you're doing pretty well as it is. The boys adore spending time with us. Do you think that would happen if they were unhappy?'

I consider this for a moment. 'But is happiness the test?'

'I want them to be happy, yes.'

'Do you think parents should have a plan – you know, for this time when their kids are starting to become independent? Starting to leave.'

'Not yet, surely,' she says with a sigh. 'They're still our little boys, aren't they?'

After a day at the beach recovering from the flights to Corfu, the boys are ready to explore the island. We decide to drive into Corfu Town for lunch and an afternoon in the old town. When, as a family, we agree that the main task of the day must be to find a good ice-cream parlour, I'm reminded that even though they're not quite *our little boys* anymore – they're both already six feet tall, in fact – they might also be holding on to something. The more protected past as part of a more demanding future, perhaps.

The thought reminds me not to settle on binaries, for the walls between stages of life, and the qualities we associate with those stages, are less fixed than that. Maybe I *am* still that young man on the back of Andreas's van, I tell myself, even if these days there's work to do to keep him in sight. I am him, as well as the father who doesn't quite trust how he went about things.

We drive up into the hills again. The sat nav that the car rental company has given me comes in different accents. We choose the Australian one. Instead of saying 'turn left', the voice tells us to 'chuck a left'. When we get to the end of the drive, he finishes with, 'Wind up your windows; you don't want those pesky seagulls eating all your chips.'

We're laughing as we do as we're told, even though we don't have any chips, and then begin our walk through the old town. Corfu has been slightly cursed by its location. It stands guard over northern Greece, is within easy reach of the other Balkan countries, and as a result has served as a watch post and fort for the naval fleets of Ancient Greeks, the Byzantines, Venetians, the

French Napoleonic empire, imperial Britain, and Nazi forces who occupied the island during World War Two.

Most of the old villages, like Karousades, are situated up in the hills, where there is more protection from raiding armies and pirates, while three forts give the capital the character of a garrison town – a place that will be fought over, and also a golden treasure of lightly coloured villas, palaces with high windows and palm trees, and ocean-front apartments with striped roller shades over their balconies.

The safety of the hilltops comes at a cost, as isolation of that kind often does. You get away from the dangers, but away from everything else, as well. These days, all the action is on the coast, and the villages are struggling to stay viable as living communities with enough facilities. In one shop, I spoke to a woman who said that there were three families still living on a permanent basis in the village where she grew up. She only went back during winter, after the tourist season. For the rest of the year, people live where the work is: in Corfu Town or by the beaches.

The result is an island with two very different characters that are nevertheless connected by the memories and movements of the people who have lived here for centuries, and always relied on both the exposure of the sea and the shelter of the hills. The Corfiots understand that it's necessary for both risk and safety to exist, even if across the generations the balance changes. I turn the thought over in my mind as we walk from the car park. How to be both, I suppose, is what they've learnt to do here – as islanders, like parents, know you *must* do. They're aware that the threats that exist out there, in the wide sea, are also where the island's life has come from.

*

Hoping to dodge the summer crowds, we make it by foot to the main fort of Corfu Town just as it's about to open and are first in line for tickets. We climb the steps to the top platform, which overlooks the entire town and two bays on either side of the town's peninsula. To the north, you can see the ferry terminal and main docks where I landed with Paul in 1990, while the southern bay is reserved for the Corfu Yacht Club and has a small pebble beach and closed-off swimming area. An enormous yacht is anchored a little out into the bay, its modern opulence and grace almost too much for the relatively diminutive appearance of the seafront buildings and park, the grandness of which is more delicate.

From the lookout, the impermanent nature of the empires that have controlled the island is evident and makes the very idea of control seem rather farcical. The boys notice the layers of history: so much can be built, only to be lost to a new force or political movement. Empires overlap, too. Below us is a structure made in the classical Greek style: a large rectangular temple fronted by Doric columns. But it was built by the British in 1840, for Christian worshippers. They wanted to connect their empire to the ones before.

'Odd combinations,' I say. 'They were part of the Pirate's nature, too. He was generous, and a menace. Funny and grumpy.'

'Smart and acting dumb,' Finnur suggests.

'Probably just drank too much of his own wine,' Magnús adds contemplatively.

I laugh. 'Right. But he wasn't exactly ever one thing or the other. I could tell he wanted to help us, and that he liked to have us around. He was a magnet for drifters and other people who didn't know what they were doing. He didn't judge anyone or turn them away. But it didn't take me long to see that he could be unpleasant, as well. Sexist. Lewd ...'

'What's *lewd*?' Finnur asks.

'You know, creepy, offensive, especially around women, and especially when he was drunk. I think that's why we never saw many women in his taverna.'

'Did you *like* the Pirate, then?' Magnús asks.

'Does it matter whether I did?'

'I reckon it does. If he was your friend, then you probably liked him in some way, right? You should just say that. In your story, I mean. You can write, *I once knew a pirate and, although he was a bit of a prick, he was also my friend.*'

I love Magnús's clarity of vision for the story, even if I don't quite share it. 'Well, he helped me when I needed help. I guess that's what I've treasured ever since, about the others who were there, too. He took me in and made me feel like I was meant to be there. There aren't many things that are more powerful than knowing you belong.'

I look into the boys' eyes to see if they understand what I'm trying to say — what I still find difficult to articulate more directly.

'After Iceland?' Finnur asks.

'Yes, after that. And, anyway, the Pirate could be fun! And he liked bringing out mountains of food, and singing and laughing and helping people to enjoy themselves. But I'm not sure we were friends.'

'You weren't *lewd*, then?' Magnús says.

'No, never! More of a romantic disposition,' I reply with mock earnestness.

'What does that mean?'

Olanda interrupts. 'It means he fell in love with every pretty girl he met.'

We're laughing now. I'm not trying to dodge Magnús's point. But I don't want the story that I tell the boys to be something other than it is. Clearer or more certain than it is. The Pirate wasn't a reformed sinner, but I don't think he was quite the scurrilous person, quite the outright pirate, he portrayed himself to be. I ask, 'Do you think it's possible to feel love towards someone you don't necessarily *like* very much?'

I wait for an answer, but they're waiting for Olanda to continue, thinking or hoping she might add some details to her definition of my romantic disposition as an eighteen-year-old. 'I'd have wanted to meet him,' she says. 'Especially at that age, when I was travelling for the first time. I wanted to be part of the world. That's what mattered to me.'

'There, you see,' I say. 'Your mum's just as odd as I am.'

'No way,' says Finnur, without feeling any need to explain why.

For a while, we trace the walls of the fort in silence, drawn into our own thoughts of the bay and the streets of the old town. Letting go. Letting *them* go, not cold-heartedly or resignedly, but with a heart full of love. To let them be part of the world. To find their own islands. That's all. It's not a *why* or *what*, I think to myself. It's *how* you cope with it. Well, how? I ask myself. For change comes whether you want it or not, and will toss all visions of control, all empires, into the sea.

The empire that put up the thick walls at which we're standing now did not think to erect a sign warning of certain death should you venture onto the walls and fall down the cliff face below. I sense the Greek antiquities authorities share this approach.

There's nothing imploring visitors to be cautious, to be mindful of their safety. Why, after all, would anyone climb a crumbling fortress wall that is a hundred feet up?

When Finnur begins to do so, I am in the process of taking a sweeping panorama that ends with footage of him ascending the wall and sliding towards its front edge.

'Hey, hey, hey,' I call out, terrified by what I'm seeing through the lens.

'What?' he says. 'Calm down.'

'Jesus Christ, Finnur. Get down.' I'm still holding the camera; the moment takes place as a weird live-action scene.

'Chill, Dad,' he says, with some disdain.

Thankfully, he turns and faces the courtyard. 'I'm down, alright,' he says, as he lands on safe ground. As we walk to the entrance of the fort, he keeps his distance from me, annoyed by my intervention, dismissing it as over-protectiveness. When he sees the wall again from the bottom, and a sheer drop that he was utterly unaware of, he changes his mind. 'Holy shit, Dad,' he says. 'What did you let me get up there for?'

9

Knowing when to go

Corfu, October 1990

I sometimes made fun of Paul for his unworldliness, his lack of
awareness. But the truth was that I had no clue what we were
going to do next, either. The perils that lay in wait for us were
concealed. But, like Finnur sitting on the edge of a fort wall, I was
drifting unknowingly towards a drop. In those situations, if you're
lucky someone grabs you before it's too late. You scramble back.

But it all seemed too good to be able to go wrong. Each day
passed the same way. We woke very early and worked until two,
rested in the afternoon or visited one of the local beaches that
were downhill from the village – Sidari; Roda, where most of
the tourists were; and the quieter Astrakeri – and then ate at the
taverna or the campground. Michelle got her quota of particulars
about us all, and in turn shared her research about the island and
its inhabitants. My favourite fact that she unearthed was that there
were four million olive trees here; they lived for centuries. They
outlasted all the empires, traders and pirates that had harassed the
island's shores. Nature was on its own timeframe.

I wasn't conscious of the island as an idea in quite the way

Michelle was. My studies focused more on the Pirate. To begin with, what I'd noticed was a well-practised restaurateur working his crowd. But the more times I visited, the more I saw how he stood a little apart from his own community, and actually sought to forge a bond with his foreign customers. The taverna's early-evening change – from a room for local customers to an attraction for foreign ones – was a daily event; his was a borderland, and he prospered on both sides, I suspected because he loved the village but also wanted to travel back to the places he'd worked as a sailor. He wanted more.

Only one of the local regulars ventured to be friends with us. His name, like a few other men in the village, was Chrisos. He was chatty, and only ten years or so older than us. He dressed in a seaside sort of way that over-advertised his looks and made him seem a bit smooth: light cotton shirts unbuttoned low down the chest, faded jeans with rolled-up hems, a gold bracelet on his wrist. One night, he offered to take us back to the campground on his scooter, one after the other. It wasn't far, but it seemed a bit too generous. When it was my turn, we wheeled quietly down the hill out of the village, and then all of a sudden he opened the throttle, and we flew the rest of the way.

I liked Chrisos, although I wondered why he was so keen to come to the campground. I thought he might want to chat up foreign girls and was using me and Paul to meet them. But that wasn't it. Night after night, he only wanted to offer advice on what to do on the island, and he didn't try anything that I could see. I realised how suspicious I was being, and mocked myself for thinking, like the local men, that it was my job to protect the girls at the campground from scooter-pirates like Chrisos.

Or I was worried that he was interested in Michelle. I had a proper crush on her now, and I thought she liked me, too. Whenever we met, she lingered longer than politeness necessitated, telling me where she'd been during the day. Her travels were still much more inquisitive than ours and her searches accumulated into a unified narrative, unfolding like the long straw mats used for paths on the beach.

Although her native language was Italian, she'd read piles of English books about Greece and the islands, their history and culture. And yet, she also seemed to appreciate my kind of engagement with Corfu, which was almost entirely through work and eating and drinking, and the information she garnered and reported to us each night. Once, while Chrisos was giving a bit of a lecture to the others around the fire, she asked me quietly about the work on Andreas's building site. She wanted to know exactly where on the island it was and what the plans were. All I could tell her was that it was further into the mountains and that my job was still just carrying. We carried cement, we carried bricks, we carried wood, we carried tools. Every day, the same. 'I feel like I've been employed on the Pyramids,' I said.

In a not swotty or superior but slightly Germanic way, Michelle said she'd written down the name of every single village and bay and beach she'd visited, even street and building names. 'I also draw them and take notes of whatever I see and learn.'

'Gosh. I draw, too, but I have trouble remembering names like that.'

'Can't you write it next to the drawing?'

'Yes, I suppose so,' I said. I didn't mind being instructed in this way, but it was strange to encounter someone who was more like me than I was.

'Did I tell you about the library?' she asked.

'No.'

'All those nineteenth-century novels were left by the same person. Someone like me, who stayed way too long and gave away all her books when she left. Helena told me. Isn't that incredible?'

'Yes. I have trouble giving away books,' I said.

'Me, too. But I'm so glad she did. Now I'm an expert in Victorian literature,' she added, jokingly. 'You said you heard of the Durrells, right?'

'Yes, Mum mentioned them to me. She loves the books.'

'You should have read them by now, don't you think? I know you like to read. What are you reading at the moment?'

'*Zen and the Art of Motorcycle Maintenance*. It was in the library.'

'I saw it too. Any good?'

I thought so, definitely. I told Michelle it was about a man who went in search of his former self, or memory of his former self, after he'd had electrotherapy that erased many of his experiences. 'He gives his former self the name of Phaedrus,' I said.

'Like in Plato?' she asked.

'Taken from Plato, yes. Phaedrus is someone he knows, and who he knows is *him*, but can't recognise as himself anymore, because he's had too much memory loss. His past is a ghost he wants to meet, and introduce to his son, too. So, they ride across America visiting the places where Phaedrus lived, thinking that maybe some of it will come back.'

'Oh, I find that spooky.'

'It makes me feel uneasy – the whole idea of the book, actually: that we have different selves that can be separated from each other.'

It may seem improbable that this could have happened: that in 1990 I read a book here about the very process I would undertake thirty years later. Retracing my steps with my sons as a way of learning together. But it's entirely true. I had found the book and couldn't put it down.

'I didn't realise you could write a creative work that was so full of open thinking,' I said. 'He spends a lot of time reflecting on his experiences.'

'Well,' said Michelle, with a smile to signal a change in tone, 'Gerald Durrell and Lawrence Durrell wrote books about Corfu. And I went to Kalami today, where they lived.' It was the village that Bella and Joe had told us about. 'The Durrells left England and found a large white house at the end of a gorgeous pebble beach. Don't you wish it was still like that?'

'Like what?'

'Don't you wish you could leave everything behind and come to Corfu and live in a house by the sea? I do. They were born in India. But their father died when they were young, so they moved to England. They couldn't stand the cold and damp and so they came here. It only went wrong because of the war. They had to leave in 1939, back to where they were *meant* to belong. That's why the books are so touching: you know what's hanging over them.'

'But Geneva isn't a hard place to live, is it?' I asked. 'Isn't it beautiful? That's what everyone says.'

'It isn't bad,' Michelle admitted. 'We have summers and real winters and proper food, not like some countries.' She giggled. 'I'm not being very nice about England, am I?'

'Paul's a bit like your Durrells. He'd do anything to get away from the rain. He doesn't mind Scottish food, though.'

'Maybe it's fine to wander around,' Michelle said. 'Never stop.'

Even if we weren't doing that at all, I thought. We were so settled here.

There was a pause in our conversation. For a moment, we listened to Chrisos vehemently insisting to someone at the campfire that he must avoid the beaches where the Germans and Swedes and English went. 'They want to make England and Germany *here*, in Corfu!' he complained. 'Gammon steaks and pints! Football. Who cares about damned football?'

'Has being here helped you?' Michelle asked me. 'You look happy.'

'I am,' I said. 'So happy. I feel like I've caught my breath.' On the island, I no longer felt winded by loss. The island had given that to me. It wasn't the same as acceptance or being reconciled to loss, but for now it didn't need to be. A rest was a gift in itself.

'Do you want to go for a walk?' Michelle said, in another of her swift turns.

'Why?'

'To look at the tress.'

'But it's dark.'

She stood up. 'Can't you see that I'm asking you to go for a walk?'

'Alright,' I said, and stood up, too.

We left the campfire. After we walked for a bit, we sat down under one of the low-hanging trees. Most likely it was an olive tree, but it was too dark to tell. Her face was close to mine.

'I can hold you, if you like,' I offered.

'Yes, hold me,' she replied and put the palm of her hand on my chest.

We sat quietly together. I thought she might tell me something about why she'd wanted to spend this time with me alone. 'What are you really doing in Corfu?' I asked when she didn't. 'Why have you been here so long?'

'Is it that hard to just hold me and not ask questions?'

I didn't mind if she wouldn't tell me, but I cared about her and what she was going through. 'Can I ask who gave you the guitar?'

'Just a friend.'

'Just a friend?'

'What's so strange about that?' she asked. 'Don't you have any friends?'

'A male friend?'

'Yes. Bravo. You caught me.'

It hadn't been my intention to do so, and perhaps she knew that as well. She took her hand from my chest, and rested her head there, and I felt her breathing, but also a sense that her friend was with us, somewhere in the shadows, in her thoughts of home. I stopped asking questions and held her. I sat as still as I could and tried to soften my breathing. 'It's okay to lose things sometimes, isn't it?' I said.

'I want to tell you something.'

'Yes?'

'I've decided that I'm going home tomorrow,' she said.

She'd been on the verge of leaving for a while, but all the same it came as a shock to hear it would be the next day. I thought about what to say. This wasn't a moment when you could tell someone that you wished they weren't leaving, was it? Even if that's what I was feeling. On an island like Corfu, meetings and partings were surely meant to be breezier than that.

'What will you do?' she asked, before I could respond.

'The Pirate says he's got more work for us after we finish on Andreas's job. He wants us to stay longer.'

'You're not going to accept.'

'I have to,' I said. 'We need more money.'

Michelle turned her face to mine and kissed me on the cheek. 'I wish I could stay longer.'

I said I'd see her again the next morning before I left for work, and we walked back to the campfire. A little later I went to bed; I felt my heart racing as I lay down, a tremulous rhythm hardened by the firm ground under the tent.

Paul heard my uneven breathing beside him. 'Alright?' he said.

'Not great at the moment. She's leaving.'

'No time.'

'Mm?'

'She didna have time for you, that's all.'

The next morning, she was still asleep when we had to go to work, and I didn't wake her. When I came back in the afternoon, she'd left for the ferry. There was a note for me. It said, *I would have liked to leave you my guitar, but I promised to give it back. Don't get stuck here. The Pirate's no good, I can feel it.*

Maybe Michelle was right. Maybe there was something very bad about him — more than mere raucousness and rancour — that was obvious to her. But I still couldn't work him out. He described himself as a sailor, but to me the circumference of the Pirate's life seemed to be limited to a kitchen and the corner table of a taverna, and at best a few dance-like steps around the other tables when he was on show, singing and expecting to be cheered on like a schoolboy breaking the rules.

On some days, it was as though he hadn't moved from where we'd left him the night before. We'd find him gazing out and I doubted whether he saw us at the front door. Was he stuck to his corner chair with his white phone, ashtray, cigarette packet and can of Coke? But then, without turning our way, he dragged himself out of his chair and lifted a hand in the air. 'Boys! Come in!'

There was no rule that said we had to go to the taverna most nights for dinner, but it was always as cheap as the first night, and the food was always as good. With Andreas's need for labour slowing, the Pirate rang around and found other work. We ploughed fields, moved furniture, painted – whatever the villagers needed. Sometimes, we would be driven up into the hills, at other times down to the fields and valleys beside the beaches, where there were still small farm holdings alongside holiday apartments and villas that were going up. We came to be recognised in the village, and entered the wave-economy of hellos, there-you-are and 'Yassou!'. Beeps.

Life was so full, bountiful, the heart so recoverable. Each week, Paul and I got fitter, healthier and more tanned; we smoked and drank less, even though we had money. By the end of October, we looked like better versions of the boys who'd left Aviemore two months before. If we kept going this way, soon we'd have enough for our bus fares to London and then some. It was working. Helena was right. The Pirate had fixed it.

Through it all, I fell more and more in love with the rowdiness and colour and smoke smell of the taverna. The blue walls were greasy in places, just like the shirts that the Pirate wore day after day. But those walls were also endlessly welcoming to whoever happened to drift past, the shelves of coloured bottles a crown of hospitality. I adored the too-loud ballads and how the Pirate joined in when a love song came on. Stumbling into the night outside into such blackness that when you held your arms out it was like you were reaching into yourself, a nothingness that existed in the deep night and its breath, the faintest breeze. A perfect endlessness.

Felix was always with us, and he and Paul and I had grown close. I learnt that Felix had lived in Karousades before. He could speak some Greek and knew a few of the villagers. One night, he also told me more about why he was here this time around, and what had happened during his military service, although as before his account seemed partial. Before the summer, he said, he'd been in a fight with his sergeant and was charged with assault. He insisted it wasn't his fault.

I listened and nodded as he spoke, but I couldn't understand how guys like him managed to get into fistfights all the time. I'd seen it every other night at the club where I worked in Aviemore. Couldn't they take a step back and see flare-ups for what they were – temporary and pretty avoidable? And yet, at the same time, I admired how he'd become part of the village, which was another expression of his strong personality. As was his relationship with the Pirate, assured and equal. Felix had fled to Corfu, but he knew how to stay and prosper here. He never doubted his right to be a dominant presence.

Once, when we came back from a job, I watched as he walked to the Pirate's table and hugged him and kissed him firmly on one of his unwashed cheeks of stubble and grease. The Pirate took the treatment placidly, and seemed to enjoy the attention, but eventually he gave one of his lazy waves to tell Felix to sit, to relax, to wait for the wine to come out.

At that moment, it seemed to me that Felix had the upper hand in their relationship, and that the Pirate was even a little in awe of his physicality and ease. Maybe even a touch afraid of him, as I think Paul and I probably were – not afraid that he was going to fight us, but that he'd drag us into the battles and other madness that he saw as ordinary.

While I watched Felix and the Pirate chat, the Pirate's mum stood beside me and rested her hand on one of my shoulders. She yell-talked at the Pirate about something in the kitchen to do with *neró*, water. He got up wearily to check what was wrong. Then, something strange happened. She began stroking my hair, gently undoing the knots that had formed from builder's dirt and sand, and from sleeping on the tent floor. She called out something to the Pirate, and I looked at him for a translation.

'Pretty hair,' he said. 'My mother says you have pretty hair. She says it is like a girl's hair.'

'Thank you,' I said, uncertainly. She patted it for a little longer. Her fingers were very thick, but she had a hairdresser's touch, or a shepherd's care with a dirty fleece. I wasn't sure how to respond, but eventually I realised no response was needed. She stroked different sections of hair, making sure each knot was fully out. After half an hour of this, with all my knots cleared up, she finished by patting me on the shoulder and walked back to the kitchen, and then came out with a basket of bread and wine.

'Drink,' said the Pirate. 'Dinner won't be ready for hours.'

It was just the three of us in the taverna, no other customers. I had time to think, and I wondered where the Pirate's father might be, and whether fatherless boys like me and Paul were more likely to end up with him. My eyes followed the line-up of empty bottles – brandy, scotch, ouzo – to the drawing of the Pirate on the back wall. He saw me looking and giggled. 'That's me.'

'Yes,' I said, 'I remember.' There the Pirate stood, setting an example to us all.

More loudly now, he said, 'I am a pirate!'

'Fuck, yeah,' I muttered, irritated.

Something had switched. Was the Pirate jealous of the attention his mother had given my hair?

I decided it was time to try to work out what he meant by *pirate*. Was he just a cartoon pirate? Or was he like Felix: ready to get into a fight at the slightest provocation, never in control of his anger? Or just a drunk old sailor who tried to be friends with boys who didn't know any better, and holding on to his youth through us? 'Why do people call you that?' I asked.

He stared at me incredulously but didn't answer and got up to fetch us more wine from the kitchen. 'Where are you from?' he asked as he came back with the bottle. He plonked it in the middle of the table, without friendliness. 'Do you live in Melbourne?'

'No.'

'I've been to Melbourne,' he said. 'Are you from Perth?' he asked next.

'No.'

'I've been to Perth. Many times.' He tried again: 'Sydney?'

'Sorry, no.'

'I have been to Sydney.' He was getting worked up. 'I have travelled a lot, yes. Do you get it? That's why I am called the Pirate. I was a sailor, like every fucking Greek guy. Sailing around, fucking around, cooking on the ships. Cooking chips. Cooking stew. Cooking, cooking, cooking. That's what we do. That's what a fucking pirate is. Do you get it now?'

I turned to Felix; he was smiling broadly, like he'd heard it before and knew what was coming next. 'Uh-oh,' he said, laughing. 'You're making him angry.'

How so? Was it against the rules to ask why people called him the Pirate?

'Where are you from, then?' the Pirate asked.

'Brisbane,' I said.

'Fuck it. I haven't been there.'

'Really?' I was a little relieved for my hometown, to be honest.

The Pirate sipped his wine. I waited for more of the outburst. But, as quickly as it had begun, it was over. Whatever I'd done to annoy him, it seemed to ease once we'd established that he hadn't visited my hometown as part of his life on the sea.

'Girls,' he said, shaking his head ruefully. I thought he was changing the subject.

'What?'

'Girls. My god. Girls.'

Felix laughed again. 'Girls. Yes!'

The Pirate grinned and poked his tongue out. His eyes opened wide. 'Pussy, pussy,' he said.

'What?'

'Pussy, pussy. All over the world.'

He pointed at the drawing again, and the woman hanging off the pirate's shoulder. She was make-believe, a cliché in a pirate sketch. But then he stuck his tongue out and giggled again, and I felt sick, Felix too, I think. We were getting the other part of his definition of piracy. 'Pussy, pussy,' he said again, and flicked his tongue around his lips. 'Hee, hee!' He laughed and raised his glass. 'I am the Pirate! Me! I am! You understand, you fucking idiots!'

*

The next day, after a few days on other jobs, we were back at Andreas's site for some final lifting and carrying he wished to be done. At lunch, he asked about our plans. He and Iris seemed worried about how things were going.

'It will start raining in a couple of weeks,' he said, 'like every November. Every year, it's exactly the same. That's why we get a lot of the building work done in the sunny weeks, when it's dry, even though it's hot. Next month, all the building sites will close. The place will be empty.'

'Where does everyone go?' I asked.

'Many people on the island have an apartment in Athens. Most of my family go there for winter. We come back in spring – April or May.'

How intriguing, I thought, for the population of an island to migrate in this way, like birds splitting the year between feeding and mating grounds. 'It's fine,' I said. 'We'll work until the rains come and then we'll find something else until it's time for us to go back to London. How much longer can you use us?' I asked.

'Two weeks, maybe a bit more,' he said.

That was bad news. I wasn't as settled in Corfu as Felix, but I wasn't ready to hear that an end point was already in sight. After all, the taverna was still doing a good trade. Every night, tourists arrived for dinner and didn't leave until after midnight. The Pirate always served the same wine that he claimed was his own and the same dinner of salty chicken that had been roasted on spits, with chips, Greek salad, peppers, tzatziki and baskets of bread. That is, nothing seemed to be changing.

*

Quite often now, we spent the night with his guests, standing in as hosts while the Pirate, the tall man and the Pirate's mum prepared the food. Around eleven one evening, a middle-aged, red-cheeked couple arrived – classic Pirate customers. They were Swedes who said they often came to Corfu for holidays, but this was their first time in the north of the island. They'd stopped at the village by chance and were sorry about how late it was. The Pirate was drunk and welcomed them warmly. 'Not too late, my friends! Come in! Where are you from? I have sailed to Sweden!'

He drew a table to alongside where the three of us were sitting. 'Sit here with my boys,' he said. *His* boys. It was the first time he'd called us that. We kept the Swedes company while the Pirate put a new round of meats on the grill. The Pirate's mum grumbled and protested, seemingly annoyed about the Pirate's willingness to start such a late service, and left for bed.

I wasn't sure why we'd suddenly become the Pirate's boys, but maybe it had been coming for a while – incremental, almost invisible steps between being taken in and being owned. It made the Swedish couple curious. They said they wanted to know about the Pirate and the taverna, and why we were there.

'The Pirate saved us,' I told them. 'We were broke when we arrived.'

'What do you mean, "saved" you?' asked the woman, Elsa.

'Gave us work around the village.'

'Are you sure *he* is saving *you*, then?' she asked. 'That's not how work is. You are the one doing him a favour. You're doing the work, right?'

'No, no,' I said. 'We were lucky to find him.'

The Swedish man, Vidar, laughed. 'A pirate and a cook.'

Felix said the Pirate was a bit rough around the edges.

He could be crude. 'But he's a kind man,' he insisted. 'He took me in as well. I don't really understand why. He likes having us around.'

I was surprised when Felix suddenly began telling the whole story of his visits to Corfu and why he was here now, completing a tale that I thought he preferred to leave unended. 'Last year, in military service, I got into a fight with my sergeant, and I hurt him real hard. I punched him and kicked him because the fucker was always pushing me, hitting me, making me do all the dirty jobs. I don't know how many times he made me clean the toilets. He hated me. I got charged with assault and they gave me a date for my court appearance. I knew they were going to give me two months, even though he was the one who did all the wrong to me.'

We sat dumbfounded by Felix's story, which was a kind of confession. I felt for him, and realised that there was bravado in Felix's confidence. Ever so slightly, a hurt boy appeared in his eyes. But he was still as matter of fact about this as everything else. 'I didn't feel like doing prison,' he went on, beginning to smile, 'so I walked out of camp and started drinking and drinking and drinking. Man, I drank so hard.'

'They let you just walk out?' Paul asked. 'That was very nice of them!'

'Yeah, I know. But that's what it was like. I knew that they were going to catch me. My friends rang me and said the police were after me. I said, "Fuck them, I want to have a good time. I'm not going to court no matter what," even though I knew they were going to catch me, and I'd have to do my time, maybe longer now that I ran away.

'So, that night I stayed out on my own drinking and waiting for them to find me, and when they didn't, I went to the red-light district and I got myself two girls and I spent the last of my money on them. I told them, "I want to have a good time tonight, because tomorrow I'm going to prison. I'm damned well sure that's what's happening!"'

My eyes must have been popping out, because Felix stopped his account and laughed at my reaction. 'You wouldn't do the same thing?' he demanded. 'Are you too pure for hookers?'

I wasn't sure of any purity on my part. But it would never have occurred to me to beat up a sergeant, skip jail and then hire two sex workers as my farewell to freedom. 'You're crazy,' I said.

'Yes! I'm a crazy fucker,' he said happily.

Paul was laughing; the Swedes, too. They weren't nearly as shocked as I was.

'Did the police get you?' Vidar asked.

'Of course. They found me at the brothel and made me go back to the camp that night. I did my time. Now I say, "Fuck the army! Fuck Austria!" They'll never see me again.'

Why was Felix telling us all this now? There must have been better ways to stop us judging the Pirate too harshly. But maybe an older couple was what he needed: his parents for an evening, to hear everything, let him explain himself properly.

'He took me in,' he went on. 'No questions. No rules. The Pirate opens his arms and says, "Let's drink!" and that's why I love him.'

For a moment, I observed the Pirate, who was still busy cooking. He was efficient, even when tipsy, and used his tiny kitchen expertly, as you might expect from a sailor. I said, 'I don't blame him for whatever part he's playing. It's his story. But that's all it is. An act that goes with the taverna.'

Felix frowned. 'Hey, idiot! You're missing the point I want to make. It's not about what he's done or what he is. I don't care if he's a pirate or a fucking vacuum-cleaner salesman. It's about who he takes in. He took me! Ja. Hmm? Would you?'

'Did he ever ask about what happened before you came here?' Vidar asked.

'Only when I wanted to talk about it,' said Felix, calming down.

'Then maybe he isn't a good *or* bad man,' Vidar said. 'He just likes to have an open door for boys like you.'

The food came out and the night wore on. Now and again, the Pirate came to check we had enough of everything. He drank and smoked with us as well, but I realised I'd never seen him eat. He must have been surviving on wine alone, waking up each morning hung over, with the memory of the day before wiped clean. Always sailing out afresh.

When we'd been talking about the Pirate, I'd noticed that Elsa didn't seem very convinced. 'Be careful,' she said to me after he left from one of his visits to our table. She was smiling, but only just. 'Don't get into trouble. I don't think you can trust him.'

Felix would have none of it. 'What can happen? We work hard, eat, drink. That's it. That's why I like it here. Everything is simple.'

Exactly. Real pirates, the dangerous kind, didn't end their days with their mothers, grilling chickens and a healthy assortment of mixed vegetables drizzled bounteously with olive oil. Real pirates didn't leave all those ports of the world for late nights entertaining Swedes and rescuing teenagers, lying about having bedded half the women of the world. 'It's alright,' I said. 'We have to go soon. The work is running out, unfortunately.'

Felix said, 'If you have any sense, you'll never leave. There's always something to do, if you know where to look. The Pirate will take care of us.'

At midnight, Elsa and Vidar paid the bill for the table and the Pirate called them a taxi. The couple hugged the Pirate and looked a bit embarrassed by how drunk they were. The Pirate's nonsense didn't seem to affect them very much. It was all a joke, a normal part of a holiday in Greece. As they left, they offered us a lift in the cab, but it wasn't far enough to bother, and we always liked the walk back to the campsite. They drove off, and Felix, Paul and I followed by foot, down the hill behind them, our arms around each other. For better or worse, we were now the Pirate's boys.

10

On the steps

'Beer for you?' the waiter asks Finnur.

His eyes dart in my direction before he answers. 'Just a Fanta Lemon,' he says. This is the closest thing to lemonade that we've found. The lovely Greek accent produces the words very quickly, but also with three *e*'s rather than one. *Leeemon.*

'Me, too,' says Magnús.

'Okay,' the waiter says. 'Two Fanta Leeemon.'

He looks a little perplexed that the boys aren't going to have a beer. I'm not sure whether it's because they look older than they are, or because there's a more relaxed attitude to drinking here, but the expectation that they'll have a drink will be repeated almost everywhere we eat. Magnús has no interest, and though Finnur does, he's also conscious of his diet, as he's in the rowing team at school: they work too hard on their fitness to let it go during the holidays.

The restaurant we've picked for lunch has its tables arrayed across a dozen wide steps of a winding lane that is hemmed in on one side by Venetian townhouses and opens to a square and garden on the other. Greek food is sometimes compared unfavourably with the cuisines of Italy and France as being too simple and homely – the qualities I love most about it. But I admit to Olanda and the boys that, since my arrival three weeks ago, I still haven't found anything that quite lives up to the Pirate's cooking.

I also know that memory can be over-generous towards the past, imbuing it with magical properties. 'I guess it was just grilled meat and salad,' I say. 'And olive oil. Lots of olive oil and lots of salt and pepper.'

Finnur has something other than food on his mind. 'Aren't you going to tell us about how you were always falling for pretty girls?' he says, suppressing laughter.

I'm sure he can tell that I'm not. It's not that the boys will tease me about how I was in the past; they're more accommodating than that. It's more that I was relieved when those years of youthful crushes came to an end. They're a part of the far past that I'm happy to leave back there. 'Are you going to tell me about what's happening in your love life?' I reply, instead.

He and Magnús simultaneously put their hands to their foreheads and sigh.

'What?' I ask.

'Did you really just say *love life*?' says Magnús.

'What am I meant to call it?'

'Don't call it anything,' says Finnur. 'Don't even mention it.' Theirs, that is.

'Well, then I'm not telling you about what I was like, either.'

'Thank god,' says Magnús.

There's a moment of quiet while the waiter comes back and lays out our cutlery and serviettes. When he's left, I say, 'Actually, my real problem was that I always seemed to be falling for the ones who didn't want to have anything to do with me.'

'Oh no,' says Magnús, 'this is going to get weird. I thought you weren't going to talk about it.' He turns to his brother. 'Did you have to ask him?'

'It's alright, Magnús,' I say reassuringly, 'it's probably good to talk about these things.'

Of course, I wasn't the first to be this way. Even then, I knew it was a cliché of romantic desire – to want what you couldn't have. A cliché that was self-defeating, too. If you kept falling for girls who didn't want you, then it was quite likely that you'd stay on your own. There was a certain dark comfort in that, a melodrama that almost felt like the real thing, a burning emotion that had nowhere to go except into your journal, and bad poetry.

The results could be also absurd. On one occasion, I was told by a friend that a girl in my class, Nadia, had a crush on me. I thought it was strange that she didn't speak to me herself, but never mind, perhaps she liked to have someone laying the groundwork ahead of that. Did I want to go on a date with her, the friend asked? I liked Nadia, but I didn't think we had anything in common, and I'd never really noticed her beyond knowing she was in a few of my classes. But I was told I should at least go out with her once. How could it hurt to go to a movie and get to know her better? So, I agreed, and the date was lovely; at one point during the movie, she turned to me and kissed me. As we left the cinema to go our different ways home, I saw how beautiful she was.

But whatever it was that Nadia had felt before our date was quenched by the evening itself, and the next time I saw her she said I was probably right, and that we weren't really a match. We could be friends, though, couldn't we? The boys will probably want to kick me from underneath the table when I say that was the moment I fell in love with Nadia, just as I fell a little more heavily for Michelle when she told me she was leaving Corfu.

I would sometimes quite like to kick my younger self, too. But, in fact, I think it can be too easy to judge the person we were in those years at the end of childhood, just as adulthood began. It's true that, as we get older, we live with the danger of nostalgia. But we also live with an equal danger that we will dismiss our younger self as entirely foolish and naive. This is to overlook what makes us *look* foolish when we're young: our openness, trust in others, disregard for danger, and willingness not to seem more knowledgeable than we really are.

In so many respects, I didn't know what I was doing, but that didn't frighten me. 'Falling in love without much success went on for years,' I go on. 'But things were different then. You know ...'

'Know what?' asks Finnur.

'Social media. The internet. DMs. We didn't have any of that. I had lots of friends who were girls. But they also seemed more distant, I guess a bit of a mystery to us. At least to me. I just sat by the phone hour after hour, willing myself to call a girl and ask her out, or hoping she would ring me. I was hopeless.'

The boys know I'm exaggerating, but all the same Olanda's heard enough and steps in to clear up the record. 'Don't believe any of this, by the way. He did *not* sit by the phone waiting for it to ring.'

'How could you know?' I say. 'You hadn't even met me then.'

'I think I know,' she replies.

'Well, I'm impressed that you had a phone,' says Finnur. 'I was imagining you sending love letters to girls by carrier pigeon.'

We laugh at this, and at an old-fashioned side of my character that is implied in Finnur's joke, as well as my age, of course. But it's true that the changes have been profound. When I was at school, we were given very little if any education about relationships, so I notice how often the boys' school gives talks about the topic. These talks emphasise open and honest communication, and respect, in particular. Sometimes, their tone has that schoolish feeling of being given a manual to follow, but I would have taken that over the silences about love and sex that existed when I was their age. 'Things are better now,' I say. 'When I was at school, we were told a little bit about the physical act of sex ...'

'Make him stop,' says Magnús.

'... things like where to buy condoms and how to put them on.'

'No more!'

'But that was it. Nothing about consent, or how to talk about sex with your partner. You were meant to intuit your understanding, but of course that just meant you went and asked your friends, who didn't know anything either.'

Among young men, the overriding principle of sex and intimacy seemed that it was either a very private matter or something for joking about. Sometimes, there would be a conversation that went beyond these two responses, both of which had the effect of closing sex off into a separate place, making it hidden. But those more open exchanges were rare and felt transgressive, as though we were in danger of being indiscreet and betraying a code that wasn't ever properly explained. Naturally, I would hate for my sons to betray the privacy of a relationship. But it's a relief to see that the topic of relationships more generally has become easier for their generation to discuss, because this is surely a way for people to be more emotionally open as well – in many aspects of life. Were they to have children, I'm sure the boys would find it utterly bemusing to imagine that, as fathers, they wouldn't be a constant part of their children's emotional development.

Our food comes out. Olanda and the boys have ordered seafood; I've chosen grilled lamb.

Finnur turns to me. 'Dad, you say you were hopeless around girls, but not everything's that different now. A lot of guys struggle to talk to girls. It's not like everything is fixed because we get a few talks at school. I know I can speak to you about this stuff, too, and that you want me to be open with you, but I still have to figure out a lot for myself.'

Of course, he's right. We're not about to find a perfect balance of privacy and openness. But I reiterate to the boys that many things weren't better back in the day. I don't want this trip to create a false idea that life is less interesting now, or less free. 'For a start, we probably wouldn't be having conversations like this,' I say.

We start eating our lunch, and for a while the conversation turns to more everyday matters. When we finish, Finnur and Magnús get up to wander around the square while Olanda and I wait for the bill. 'Do you think you would have been any different with Michelle?' she asks. 'If it was happening now, I mean.'

I give it some thought. 'I think I would have tried harder to understand what she wanted from me. She was struggling with something, a loss. I can see now that I could've worked it out sooner than I did. I didn't really get it until she was about to leave, and then I wasn't much use.'

'You don't know that for sure,' says Olanda. 'There was something there that was helpful to both of you.'

Olanda and I met a full ten years after I'd been to Corfu, when I was twenty-eight. By then, I was a postgraduate student writing a doctoral thesis about medieval Icelandic literature. We met on campus. She was working for the university travel agency, and I was buying a ticket to Reykjavík. It was true that I still fell for pretty girls, if not quite as easily as when I was in Greece. But I felt very lucky when I saw that Olanda would be my travel consultant. When, a few weeks later, I had to go back to change the date of my flights, her arm was in a sling. She said she'd hurt it skiing and was pretty housebound at the moment. Without thinking about it fully, I asked her if she was well enough to go to the movies. My stomach dropped as I waited for her response. But she smiled and said yes. Movies were still a possibility, even with a fractured bone.

Our waiter still hasn't returned; he seems to be having a fight with his iPad. It gives me time to ask Olanda what she thinks of the conversation we've been having with the boys, before we ate.

She says the main thing for her is that the boys seem comfortable talking to us. 'But we have to know they're not always going to feel that way. They'll make their own mistakes. That's when they'll need to be able to come to us, knowing we'll be there without judgement.'

'The main thing we do is listen?'

'Something like that. I remember I always wanted to be more open about relationships with my parents, but they couldn't really cope with that. After I had my first proper kiss, I wanted to talk about it with them, but it was just awkward. They said, "Oh, that's nice," and that was it. They never said any more about it.'

'Do you think they wanted to?'

'I'm not sure,' she says. 'And isn't part of it about gender, in that moment when I wanted to speak to them? It's such a change that young men are now encouraged to talk about emotions, experiences. And that's going to bring about changes in their first relationships, too. For them as well as their girlfriends. They can listen to each other, as equals.'

The ability to listen. It sounds like such a simple act: staying quiet for long enough to let someone reveal their side of things. But if you did it often enough, people would see that you knew how.

The idea reminds me that I really only glimpsed Michelle's story. But she'd written that she hoped I wouldn't get stuck in Corfu, as perhaps she almost had. She seemed to know that at some point you had to accept that the season was over, and you had to return to your life before it: this reprieve couldn't go on forever.

11

Offers of piracy

Corfu, November 1990

The following week, the autumn rains arrived, just as Andreas said they would. It wasn't heavy rain, and it was still warm, but the clouds and the steady drizzle that they brought changed the island. The colour of the sea became rock-like and shadowy, the green of the forests and olive groves sank a little into the baser browns and greys of the hills. I enjoyed seeing the landscape and the villages adjust to autumn, and it wasn't a terrible thing that the tourist resorts and towns were quiet. The beaches emptied, and we swam alone in rain-calmed seas, the stony Albian hills seemingly raised even higher in the less-blanching light of November. But the money was leaving along with the sun.

By the end of the first week of that month, Paul and I were the only ones left at the campground. Felix had found a mysterious attic room for himself in the village; the rent was next to nothing. Then, Helena said it was time for her to close. She was sorry, but we'd need to find somewhere else. She suggested asking the Pirate. He knew everyone; he'd find us a room.

When we brought it up with him one morning, he shook his

head and said there was no need to rent from anyone else. He had a villa! It wasn't quite finished yet, but it was on the beach. It wasn't being used. Each of us could have a room for the equivalent of two dollars a night. 'Is that okay?' he asked.

'Yes, very okay,' I said.

'Then you stay there. It is a favour to me. I will know there is someone in the house. That's good for me. Everyone gets what they need.'

The Pirate's villa was a long, English-style bungalow a few steps back from Astrakeri beach, two kilometres downhill from the village. Astrakeri wasn't one of the famous beaches of Corfu; it was still home to a mix of farms, empty fields with rubbish on the fringes, and fishing shacks. The Pirate must have thought it would pay off eventually, and he was slowly building it so that it would be ready for the magical day when the beach was discovered. But there was also a strange law in Greece that Chrisos had explained to me: you didn't pay tax on a building until it was finished, so maybe it would stay unfinished forever.

When we arrived, we saw that the villa was still a long way from completion. Builder's rubble was piled up in what should have been the garden. There was a half-built bar in the living room, a hole in the ground for a spa bath to go in. The rooms were unfurnished except for a bed in each; the lighting cables were exposed, with bulbs dangling from the wires. Two working lamps in each room, so at least there was light.

Paul and I took rooms at opposite ends of the house, like something you'd expect of a married couple who'd fallen out of love. We didn't bicker or tease each other in the way we'd done when we were travelling and feeling broke and vulnerable. As things had grown quieter on Corfu, we could see that we'd grown apart, as though we'd had different experiences of the island, however similar they seemed on the surface. Our conversations were turning civil. Before the campsite closed, we'd rented scooters for a day, and twice I watched him slide off the road and scratch the side of his scooter in the gravel. I yelled at him to ride straight, not to lean into the corners as much. It was a miracle that we weren't fined for the damage; maybe the hire company didn't see the marks. But that he couldn't stay upright annoyed me so much more than was fair – he just couldn't ride a scooter very well.

At night, we often left the taverna at different times. Paul always stayed on with Felix and the tourists drinking late, but I was starting to get bored by these sessions, and I left earlier and walked back on my own.

The lane down to Astrakeri came off the main road, near another taverna that didn't get much business; it was more like a corner store than a restaurant. The villa was only fifteen minutes' walk away, but the lane was steep and dark: there were few streetlamps, and they didn't always come on, and the olive groves and fields and vines on both sides absorbed and concealed any night light there might be.

I started to dread those evening walks. In such moments, I was no longer part of the group, one of the Pirate's boys. I liked being on my own, but the back roads felt unsafe at night. I imagined some malice in the shadows. Now and then, I heard shepherdesses groaning from farm sheds. They gave miserable, lonely utterances that seemed like a response to my footsteps. Maybe it was singing or talking, but I couldn't distinguish it from the morbid wailing you'd expect from ghosts. Dogs snarled and pulled on their chains. I was convinced one would escape and attack me. Where was Paul,

I groaned to myself. Why weren't we looking out for each other anymore? Where was the Corfu of our arrival?

With the sound of the sea at the end of my walk, my spirits lifted. There were stray dogs on the beach, too, but they weren't territorial and didn't bark. It was open, and the night sky was lighter by the water. I was able to slow down and enjoy my last steps to the villa. I thought about how things were changing on the island very quickly, and how easily we'd returned to the beginning – relying on favours and kindness. We were stranding ourselves once again.

With the arrival of the rains, the work on the building sites ceased for winter, and, as Andreas had forewarned, many of the builders and farmers and villa owners left for Athens. We began to get days in a row of no work. On one, we caught the bus to Corfu Town and spent a morning happily wandering the streets. It was the first time since we arrived that we'd had a proper look.

We strolled through the old town, reading plaques and booklets. The people of Corfu claimed that Odysseus had stopped here and that his descendants walked the pavements of where the town was, for Odysseus, like the Pirate, seemed to manage to have affairs whenever he visited a new place.

'That's what he told everyone, anyhow,' Paul joked. 'Why aren't *we* getting any sex?'

'Maybe we're not heroic enough,' I offered as a suggestion.

Paul frowned. 'You think we're pretty shit, don't you?' he said, his voice filled with acrimony. It wasn't really how he was as a person, but maybe he sensed that things were coming to an end.

I noticed that even the main town of the island was quiet, as though we'd arrived in the last hour before closing time. Back at the taverna, even the local men who came by for their afternoon drink seemed to begin leaving the island. Over three more days, we didn't get work. Not only were we not saving, but we were also going backwards, and I had to empty out our savings just to keep us fed. Soon, we were going to be completely broke.

We were relying too much on the Pirate. He provided everything: food, work and accommodation. He said we were his boys. I wondered if I would start to become more and more like him, and like Felix, failing to see the peril in the life of escape they wanted – how it blunted the emotions, even if it opened a door to adventures.

A ledger was set up with the Pirate. It was monetary but also ethical, a life. I was joining some kind of pirate band. And, as quickly as the ledger was running, we weren't paying the four dollars we owed the Pirate per night for the villa, or for our meals and wine. He said not to worry. We could pay him later. But when would that be? In the spring, when people started coming back? How would we earn anything before then?

After a whole week without work, I confessed to the Pirate that I was worried. 'Work for me, then,' he said. 'I'll take your pay off the villa and dinners. Off the ledger. You don't have to worry. There's lots to do. Always.' He told us to be at the taverna at nine the next morning. 'We don't have to start as early as the builders.'

I thanked him for whatever work he could give us. The Pirate was surely able to 'fix it', just as he had when we first arrived. I said we'd see him in the morning at nine, not thinking to ask what the work would be.

*

We'd been living in Karousades for six weeks now, but in all that time I'd never seen the Pirate outside the taverna door. It gave me a shock. Standing in the narrow street, he didn't look like himself at all: he seemed shorter and more crumpled, less of the character he played. I realised that he was scaled perfectly to squeeze himself into the narrow gaps between the taverna's tables.

He was already annoyed about something; I couldn't tell what. He yelled out to Paul and me, ordering us to wait by the taverna door, and after a few minutes he appeared in a small red car. This surprised me even more. It didn't occur to me that he'd own a car and drive around the island. Was he a normal person? No, he wasn't normal. He was different, possibly even better than all the respectable people who wouldn't dream of taking in penniless travellers. I knew Andreas was a more upstanding man than the Pirate, but his hospitality had limits and boundaries. The Pirate wasn't like that at all. His openness was all-consuming. And now he had moving legs and a car and we were off.

As we left the village, the Pirate said again that he'd put our wages for the day against the rent we owed him, seeing as the ledger was building up. We followed back roads to his olive farm, a short drive from the village. He said, 'You will lay the nets we use to catch the olives when they are ripe.'

The Pirate's land was hilly, dry and uneven, and setting out the black wire was awkward. The netting caught on boulders and roots, and it was hard to keep your balance on the rocks and the steeper parts of the hill. The Pirate watched us from the top; he didn't seem very keen on moving from where he stood. But, even from that distance, he could see we weren't doing a good job.

'Roll them out gently,' he yelled, with a cigarette in his hand. 'Smooth!'

Instructing us to be better at the job didn't help. We were trying our best to keep the netting smooth, but every time one of us laid the net down, the other end became uneven or tangled. Eventually, the Pirate came down a few steps and demonstrated on an upper section. He pulled on the net while Paul tried to flatten the sides. 'Don't stand on the nets. Don't leave bulges. No rips!'

We tried and tried without him, but it was hopeless. The Pirate was losing it. He walked further down the hill and evened out the sections we'd tried to do. 'This is total shit,' he said. 'I will have to do it all again.'

Just then, another car arrived at the top of the hill. It seemed the Pirate had been expecting it, as straight away he waved at the driver and started to climb back up the slope. 'Here,' he said to us. 'Come with me.'

We made our way towards an old farmhouse on the property. It didn't look like anyone had lived there for years; as far as I knew, the Pirate only ever slept in an apartment above the taverna. He was angry with us about the nets and didn't have anything to say.

Two lads were waiting for us beside the car. They spoke to the Pirate in Greek and stared at us. One of them carried a large white bucket, a length of rope and a set of knives.

The Pirate led us to a second, much smaller, building: a lime-coated outhouse that sat to the side of the farm. When we reached the door, I saw an enormous pig standing forlorn inside, and I began to suspect what was coming next. It was as if the pig could sense the violence as well, in a ghastly stillness that was all fear. I felt that the pig wasn't at all resigned to its death, that it was still hoping for a change in what was happening.

The room was cold, the space only a little bigger than a bedroom. It had a cement floor that was already wet; maybe one of the lads had washed it down. Or had the Pirate moved the pig here when we were putting out the nets? That I couldn't remember seeing him leave gave the moment the air of a secret killing, gang-like and shameful.

A sledgehammer rested against the wall. The Pirate lifted the tool and offered it to me, also pointing at the pig. Paul and the two lads waited for me to take it. I shook my head. 'I don't want to kill it,' I said.

'Why?'

'I don't know how to.'

The Pirate pointed at his forehead. 'Hit it there,' he told me. 'Hard.'

I turned to Paul. 'I'm not doing it,' he said.

The Pirate shook his head. 'Total shit,' he said again.

He crouched a little, steadied himself. Then he struck the pig square across the temple with a single, ferocious blow. It was awful. The poor animal screamed; it was a bewildered and shrill cry, filled with horror. Rank fear. A second later, it fell to its side, kicking on the floor. Yet again, the Pirate was transformed from whom we had known in the taverna – he now seemed younger and completely capable. He put down the sledgehammer and took hold of one of the butchering knives the lads had brought. He bent over the pig and lifted its head so that it was facing us. Then, he pushed the tip of the knife into its throat and cut across the neck swiftly and assuredly, and the pig's head flopped back, like the top of a suitcase, dead.

The Pirate handed the blade back to one of the lads. They stepped forward and strung the pig by its hind legs to a hook in the ceiling and put the white bucket under its neck to collect the blood.

Paul and I didn't move. I felt sickened, not least by myself. It was such an ugly thing to stand by and watch, as a boy might – not knowing how to stop it, or even that I had the right to walk away. I didn't want to see it; I should have left when I realised what was happening.

The Pirate wouldn't have stopped me. But it was too late now.

How awful to be led along like this.

Out of nowhere came a packet of yellow disposable razor blades. The Pirate gave me and Paul one each. He sprayed oil on the pig's skin and lit it with his lighter. The pig's hair caught fire, and then curled and browned. He told us to start shaving. We could manage this: finally, we were able to do a task we'd been given. When the hair was gone, the innards were taken out and placed in the blood bucket, and the carcass was moved across to a waist-high table for butchering. The lads did this: they packaged the meat for the Pirate to take to the taverna.

We drove back in silence. I still felt nauseated, and unbelieving of what had happened. Paul was white as a sheet, too. But now that we neared the village again, the Pirate became chattier, relieved to be back, I thought. He started to resemble himself again, the taverna host rather than the man who in a matter of two swift movements squatted and bludgeoned an animal.

After we'd carried the meat into the taverna, the Pirate sorted it into parcels for storing and freezing. The Pirate's mum took a cut of bacon and sliced it thickly and cooked it for us. When she brought it out with bread and coffee, she began, as she had before, to stroke my hair. It wasn't creepy, but it felt very odd after the morning we'd had. I had no reason to think this, but for a moment I imagined her calming me in preparation for slaughter, for the Pirate's sledgehammer against my forehead.

Out of nowhere, Felix appeared. There was something weird about that, I thought: like he'd been told to come, and Paul and I were unwittingly part of a pre-scripted morning, just as when the local lads arrived unannounced with the butchering equipment. Something was going on.

The Pirate's mum's stroking continued.

The Pirate came out from behind the counter and said he wanted to speak to us about a big job. He sat us around the table nearest the end wall, which had a bench as well as chairs. The three of us sat on the bench while he took his own seat. The Pirate's mum had stopped at last.

'You are my boys,' he said. 'You are good boys and I like you. Like sons. You are my sons. Now I'm going to tell you about my winter work. I will take my boat to Athens. Then we go to South America. This winter I want the three of you to come with me. You will be part of my crew. I will pay you, of course.'

'Okay,' said Felix, delighted. 'Where will we go?'

'Brazil.'

'Brazil?' cried Felix.

'Don't yell,' said the Pirate. He smiled at Felix's disbelief. 'It is the best country in the world. Better than all the other countries put together. Oh my god, Brazil.'

'We're going to Brazil,' Paul exclaimed.

Was he mad? I stared hard at him to shut him up. We couldn't just agree to sail to Brazil. The Pirate, though, seemed to think that the deal was settled, all in a matter of two minutes.

He left the table to fetch wine. Paul and I looked at each other but couldn't speak. When the Pirate came back, Felix asked for more details. 'What do we do in Brazil?' he asked.

I think we were all hoping the Pirate would say that he

wanted to ship his olives or wine or even pig meat. Begin a Greek taverna in Rio. But he wouldn't be drawn, not yet. 'Don't worry about that,' he said. 'I will tell you when we leave. It is things they need there.'

Need? Was the Pirate a smuggler? I supposed he already was. What were we three, if not smuggled goods brought in through his door and passed around the work sites?

He held his glass and took a contemplative sip. 'One thing you must know, boys,' he said. 'Are you listening?'

'Yes,' I said.

'There is one rule of life on the sea. If you don't get on with the other crew, we push you in.'

'In?'

'Into the sea. Dead.'

We stayed quiet, and again I felt like I was the pig being readied for slaughter. He added, 'I mean it.'

Then, perhaps as every pirate, real or pretend, must do at least once in their life, he held up his index finger and with it drew a line across his neck. He chuckled. 'Don't look so worried. We have a good time. I will take care of you. I will be your father and you will be my sons!'

12

Small acts of acceptance

In Icelandic, there are words for the relationship of father and son, and that of mother and daughter. These are *feðgar* and *mæðgur*. Separate words also exist for the father–daughter and mother–son relationships: *feðgin* and *mæðgin*. They seem to acknowledge the distinct nature of these relationships, and some element of joint identity that exists in them. *Feðgar* means 'father and son', while also capturing a distinct idea of their togetherness.

The Pirate wasn't the first person who offered to be my father, or, in his case, declared himself as such. Husbands of Mum's Icelandic girlfriends, an uncle on my father's side, various colleagues of Mum's, the Englishman who wanted more discipline for me, and even Mum's ex-husband from before she met my father had all offered to be registered as my legal father, even if they weren't my biological one. Such was the affection that people had for my mother, and such were the prevailing attitudes to single-parent families.

Because of its very rural roots, Iceland is a country where people are used to having two or three jobs or roles. This means that grandparents have a prominent role in raising children; even though the country has changed a lot in the past decades, it seems to me that that aspect of family life hasn't altered very much. And so, though fathers were present, they were also often less involved in day-to-day parenting than they are today. At the same time, they were also seen as indispensable.

I find myself wondering why: I'm curious to know what the more distant or always-at-work model of fatherhood was thought to give children, the part that couldn't be replaced by other relationships. The unique property of fatherhood. A different kind of authority? Gender balance? Instruction in the things men usually liked doing and women didn't? Perhaps it was as difficult to pin it down, as changing, as it is now. But I do know that Mum saw a need as well. She liked her male friends, and male company more generally: what she felt were their open, non-judgemental ways. She thought it was important to have that in my life.

But as much as it might seem a strange thing to say, I love that Mum gently declined the offers of formal or legal paternity that she received, and that she chose not to replace her silence about the true identity of my father with a kind of falsehood. That sounds harsher than I mean it to be. There was never any intention to deceive me, and some of these men did become valuable father figures for me. It wasn't so much what they did, although that mattered, too – they took me fishing, gave me jobs to do, brought me to their workplaces, let me steer a boat, and taught me how to stack hay on their family farms. Talked to me about sport and cars. More important than any of these individual things was how they formed a chain of small acts of acceptance. I didn't doubt Mum's care for me, but when I spent days with these father figures, I was offered a very particular form of acceptance, one that emerges silently, to the side of what's going on in front of you, from people with whom you simply share a way of being. The closest analogy I can think of is a musical beat that you recognise and can join, almost without thinking – a part of the music that also stands behind it.

I didn't ever want a replacement for my actual father. For me, the relationship of *feðgar* was not divisible in that way, even if my father wasn't in my life. To have accepted a new father would have meant closing a door that I wanted left open for him – an open door that has no doubt helped to shape me. A friend of mine, a fellow writer, sometimes tells me that what he sees as my ambition and creativity might be the result of *not* having a father in my life. He suggests that my father's absence, combined with my life as a migrant, has given me something of an outsider's perspective that, I admit, is also bound up in who I am as a writer. Outsiders sometimes have to search a little harder before they fully understand what's going on, which after all is what writers also do.

I now see that when the Pirate said he was going to be my father – and we, his sons – it expressed something of what he'd already shown me: friendship and affection, an acceptance of who I was, and an interest in me. I was very grateful for that. The Pirate had offered this to strangers and stragglers, a group of boys he recognised as fatherless. Maybe it was because he was also fatherless at that point in his life: just him and his mother running the taverna, living side by side, day after day. But whatever the reason, the Pirate knew how to make us feel that we were okay as we were and could stay as long as we liked.

After lunch, we stroll through the tight shopping streets and lanes of the old part of Corfu. Most of this area of town is set aside for tourist shops and restaurants. There's a lot of leather and woodwork from olive trees, sandals, marble and gems. The Italian influence is everywhere, too, in the ice-cream parlours, the languorous glamour of the young, the purposeful leisure of coffee-shop conversations, the smell of wine and bread.

Olanda and I decide to buy a couple of cushion covers to take back to Brisbane, one for us and one for Mum. The pictures on them are exactly what you'd expect of a Greek cushion cover: a scooter leaning against the front of a whitewashed house, olive trees camouflaging a farmhouse in the hills. I want the boys to buy something local to take home, too, but they're less taken with the touristy goods, and would prefer to go to the Adidas shop instead. Quite probably, the cushion covers are from as far away as the sports T-shirts they end up finding.

By then, it's becoming much hotter, and the streets are crowded, and the sweetness of the morning is evaporating. We stroll back up to the car, passing a high school on our way. The school year has just begun here, and I notice the boys very deliberately avoiding eye contact with the girls who are looking out of the window at them, and who seem to want to say hello.

'Don't say a word,' Magnús tells me.

'I wasn't going to.'

'Dad,' says Finnur, 'we mean it.'

'Well, maybe I was going to say that you should give those girls a wave, seeing as they're trying to say hi to you.'

'They aren't.'

'No, look,' I go on. 'I think they're trying to get your attention.'

'I swear, Dad ...' says Finnur.

Unsurprisingly, the boys walk a little faster now, quite some steps ahead of me and Olanda, and we don't catch them until we're all back at the scratched Renault hatch. On the drive to Karousades, we chat about Corfu Town and our impressions from the day, but soon we're back to thinking about the village and the Pirate. I'm surprised to hear the boys say that they're keen to get back to the story.

I tell them about how things started to change on the island after Paul and I moved to the Pirate's villa and began to rely on him more.

'Did you see you were getting into trouble?' asks Finnur.

'I think it had felt too good to go wrong. I didn't realise a place could change as quickly as Corfu did: one minute it was busy, the next moment everyone had left. And I really did trust the Pirate. I could tell that he was fond of us and wanted to keep helping.'

'And he never had children of his own?' Olanda asks.

'Not that he ever mentioned. It's hard to believe, I know.'

'If all that stuff about the women in his life is true.'

'You doubt it's true?'

'I didn't know him. But sometimes, when you describe him to us, it reminds me of how some people with depression or anxiety talk about their lives. How his mornings were very bad, and he seemed really dark, and found it hard to get going. Then, eventually, he got some rhythm from his work, from getting into the day, getting the restaurant ready. And, at night, he looked for happiness in the crowded taverna, and in drinking hard. If it was the same every day, it sounds a bit like he was trapped.'

'And yet, despite all that, he managed to adopt us.'

'Yes. But I would say that you helped him. I don't think you should underestimate what you were giving back.'

Perhaps Olanda's right: I think of the affirmations of the *feðgar* relationship, and how they move in more than one direction and even across time. Being Finnur and Magnús's father has given me a sense of purpose and a feeling of acceptance that is oddly similar to what I hope to give them. Often, all I really needed from the men I knew when I was a boy was to be allowed to stand around and listen, to have a presence and maybe say the odd word. In the same way that, now, the boys and I often don't look for much more from each other than that feeling of being present in each other's lives.

At their best, such moments are rather like the feeling you get when you're travelling with someone and you've reached the point when there's no need to say anything. A comfortable silence, I suppose, that is punctuated by observations and stories, instructions and requests, but is also enough in itself, because the shared task of the journey has developed its own rhythm, its own beat that sits behind the notes.

13

The first debt

Corfu, November 1990

That night after we had flayed the pig, I lay in bed remembering the Pirate with his long butchering knife, squatting low. I imagined my own pink face braced between his knees as he went in for the kill. We'd completely misread him from the beginning. He *was* a pirate. The play-acting of piracy was a cover for actual piracy, and I was going to end up on a creaky smuggler's boat bound for Brazil, tethered to the mast if I did anything wrong, or cast into the ocean if I didn't *get on with the crew,* whatever that meant. Would they be patting my long hair in the way that the Pirate's mother liked to?

It's over, I told myself. *We have to get away.*

Every morning, clouds continued to block the east sky and bring only more rain and less chance of new work. We persevered with walking up to the bench outside the taverna in the hope that one of the builders might need workers. We sat there for an hour or two, no-one came, and then we went back to the villa. We'd spent most of the money we'd saved. Between us, we were down to ten thousand drachmas in cash – about a hundred dollars – and we now owed the Pirate six thousand drachmas for food and the villa.

As we walked back down the hill one morning, I asked Paul what he thought we should do next. In his mind, there was no choice but to join the Pirate on his trip to Brazil. 'Where else would we go?' he asked. 'There isn't anything for us in Athens. And after Athens, it's back to London, or Scotland. I'm not leaving this. Not yet.'

'But we *would* be leaving this,' I said. 'The Pirate wants us to go to Brazil.'

'Not this,' he said. 'Not all *this*.'

'What?' I yelled. 'What the hell do you think we're doing?'

He thought about it for a moment. 'You fuck off then. You go back. I told you, I'm not leaving. I'm not stopping you, am I? Couldn't care less what you do, you tosser.'

I lowered my voice. 'How are you going to get by on your own?'

'You don't think I can manage?'

'Paul, we both know you can't manage. How much money have we got? C'mon. Tell me. Do you even know? Do you care?'

'Not this again. All you think about is money.'

'Sort of, yes. I think about food and warmth and weird shit like that.'

He stormed off to his end of the villa, his side of a divide that I didn't want. We did need each other – to get out of this situation, just as we'd needed each other to get into it. And, as my mind worried over how we'd cope, I could guess where Paul's thoughts lay.

When I first met Paul, in Aviemore, he mentioned he was getting away from some troubles that he had in Glasgow. I'd assumed he meant money trouble. Aviemore was the sort of place that collected runaways, much as Corfu did. It was a resort town, and no-one knew anyone else's backstory. It didn't bother me at all.

But when I came back from my trip to Iceland and met up with Paul in Glasgow, he took me to visit his family, and there he gave me the fuller picture of what he'd left behind.

We stayed at his mother's small townhouse. Like me, Paul didn't know his father, who'd died when he was very young. I often became friends with people who had stories like that, even though I usually didn't find out until some way into the friendship. People without fathers often had a common approach to life, a less certain perspective, that sought out other people like them.

When we were planning our trip, he sometimes said he'd do whatever he could to get away and have a more exciting life; he didn't want to die without seeing the world first. He kept repeating that he was sure he'd never get another chance, and that our friendship, my arrival in his life, was a sign that he should travel now or regret it forever. I thought this was a strange way for him to talk, given that he'd only just turned nineteen. He had years ahead of him for travelling. But one evening while we were at his mother's place, his ex-girlfriend Leah popped in for a visit, along with their daughter, Chloe, who'd just turned one.

Leah saw the expression on my face. 'He didn't tell you, did he?' she asked.

'No, he's never said.'

She turned her child on her lap so that they were facing each other. 'Well, our Paulie's a da, isn't he, darling?'

All that night, Paul was captivated by his daughter and couldn't do anything except play with her. Chloe didn't resemble him, exactly, but she was a beautiful little girl who smiled all the time, just like he did: they shared his constant cheekiness and desire to laugh. It was obvious he'd missed her while he was living in Aviemore. I'd never seen him as happy or as focused on one person. He seemed a natural father, though he'd kept it to himself.

During the two days that followed, his family was lovely to me. In the evenings, they ordered fish or fried ribs dinners from the local fish-and-chip shop, and Paul's brother and friends took me to play pool at the ex-servicemen's club nearby. It was all laughter and jokes. But it was impossible not to feel how disappointed they were that he was leaving. Their kindness didn't conceal the fact that they saw me as another one of Paul's mistakes in life.

I asked his mother if I could store my suitcase in a closet under the stairs. I really disliked the thing, and I didn't want to pull it through Europe. She agreed, and the next day Paul and I caught a bus into Glasgow centre to buy rucksacks to take instead. 'Why didn't you tell me about Chloe before?' I asked him on the way. 'We've known each other for long enough, haven't we? I don't keep things from you.'

'People don't understand,' he said. 'I was only seventeen when Leah fell pregnant. What am I meant to do? It didn't work out.'

'Don't you think you should stay, seeing as your daughter's here?'

'I will. I need this first,' he said. 'I never had a pa,' he added, and hit me on the leg – affectionately, I thought. 'Your da doesn't even want to see you again! We've turned out alright, haven't we?'

I'd nodded, but my heart sank, as it did now, while Paul was in the other room, angry with me for trying to end his escape from Glasgow, and from fatherhood and his own adulthood, I suppose. I didn't think it was up to me to tell Paul how to be a father. But I suspected part of him wished he could live in Glasgow so that he could be close to his daughter. He often took out a picture of her. I hoped he was looking at it now.

I walked down the corridor to his door and knocked. 'Are you in there?'

'Of course I am, you dickhead,' he answered.

'Are you coming out any time in the next little while?'

'What for? So you can tell me how to live my life?'

'Something like that,' I said.

He pulled the door open and sat back on his bed. 'Come in, then.'

'The Pirate *is* a pirate,' I said. 'Are you?'

'No, I'm not a pirate, Kári,' he said, 'any more than you are. We're a pair of fucking ninnies.'

I told him how it would go. The voyage to Brazil would start alright, and we would be the Pirate's boys and he would be our father, promising protection and money, going on about how he knew all the beautiful women of Rio. 'Right?'

'Aye, that's it.'

'Then, one day, he'll want something done, something unpleasant, and it'll be the olive nets and the pig kill all over again. We'll be just as hopeless and disgusted, but this time his anger will have nowhere to go but at us, and we'll be thrown overboard, fed to the sharks of the southern Atlantic. Didn't you see how he killed that pig? He could kill anything. Anyone. Us!'

'I still think that's a pile of shite, Kári. He's just trying to scare us. He's a sweetie. He wants to help. Are we not enjoying his hospitality and good grace in the villa? Does he not feed us every night?'

'It's a trap,' I said. 'Why isn't he telling us more about the trip? What the hell is he taking in a boat to Brazil?'

'He must be at the planning stages,' Paul suggested.

'What if it's drugs? Or guns?'

'Or something nice and innocent, like olives. Bacon, even.'

I noticed that Paul had the photo of Chloe partly concealed under the bedding. 'What's that picture?' I asked.

'I think you know. Leave it for a bit, would ya? I'll cordially notify you of my decision when I've made it.'

The Pirate, for his part, had assumed that it was all settled, and began to sketch out a timeline. 'We go in two weeks,' he said one afternoon. 'To Brazil!'

We had stayed on, idle but still somehow convinced that we could get work and pull ourselves out of the pit into which we were sliding. We had begun to borrow extra money, too – just small amounts from the Pirate, enough for the rent, beer, cigarettes and meals. We needed to make a decision. A simple one: to become pirates or not.

I tried to bring it up with Paul again, but he wasn't having it. 'I'll tell you if I ever receive a revelation,' he said.

For now, each morning, it was the same pointless routine, walking from the villa to the taverna and back again, morning and evening. On one of these nights, I got bored of the taverna and told Paul I was leaving early, even before we'd eaten. Paul asked me to leave my wallet. There wasn't anything unusual about that. If one of us was staying at the villa, the other would take the money. I took a thousand-drachma note to buy myself some snacks and beer on the walk home and left Paul with the rest, our last funds.

I stopped at another taverna, the one that doubled as a corner shop, and picked up a packet of cheese and some bread. When I'd returned to the villa, I poured myself a glass of beer and opened the cheese, broke off a piece and swallowed it.

The first thing I knew was that it was the worst taste I'd ever experienced, a vile, deathly flavour, as though I'd bitten into a carcass. Rotten. Then, I realised I'd swallowed some of it, too: a morsel just before I could spit the rest out. A few minutes later, I began to vomit. I tried to drink a glass of water but couldn't keep it down. I vomited again. A few minutes later, again. It came out in uncontrolled gushes that splashed around me before I could get to the bathroom.

I crawled to the toilet bowl and waited for more vomit to come. By that point, I was already too weak to stand. My head spun and my legs were shaking. Until midnight, I vomited every ten minutes, until my stomach was completely empty; all I could produce was a painful dry retching.

My eyes watered. I was dizzy and starting to worry that it was more than just food poisoning. What the hell was in that cheese? Was I dying? And where was Paul? It was after midnight and there was still no sign of him. I needed his help to get back to the taverna, to get to a doctor. Why did he choose this moment to go missing?

I managed to stand up and make my way to the door but, before I could reach it, I fell and began dry retching on the floor. I was losing control at the other end as well, but the faintness and nausea were so bad that I couldn't sit on the toilet. My body was willing to destroy itself to get the cheese out. I groaned and leant against a wall. 'I'm screwed,' I muttered.

All night, I waited for Paul. But by dawn, he still wasn't back. I spent the morning dry retching and trying to sip water. It didn't work; nothing stayed down. My head ached and I didn't think I could walk. My heart ached as well. I felt the weight of the months I'd been abroad. All that bullshit about trusting the road. Look where that got you. Lying in your own spew and shit.

Where the hell was Paul? Dead? On a boat to Brazil? Did he and the Pirate and Felix leave without me? Would they do that? Had they picked me as the one they'd have to throw overboard anyway?

Kill me now, I thought. *Get it over with.*

My head whirled, my thoughts ever darker. Why had I left Brisbane, my beautiful paradise home, just to wander the haunts of all that was over, all that was gone? What was my father to me? A pirate, a ghost ship of a man who couldn't bring himself to love his son. It didn't matter. I was a man now. He was the past, a relic, and there was nothing left to find or even search for, not here in rotten, ancient Europe. Not in miserable, closed-up Iceland. A country as hostile as my stomach, spitting its children out.

Ugh. I tried to shake myself out of it. It was stupid lying on the floor, thinking such idiotic things. I couldn't stay in the villa. I needed help. I needed to find the strength to drag myself up the hill, possibly past Paul's decomposing body, to somewhere people could see me and tell me what to do.

I waited until there was a gap in the vomiting and, at noon, I staggered up to the village. The rain held off. I shuffled up at half the pace of the old men and women you sometimes saw, bent over, fetching things from the shops. I stopped every dozen paces to catch my breath. But I made it to the top of the hill and into Karousades.

There was only one place I could think to go. The taverna. Not to a doctor, but to the Pirate. That decision seems so revealing to me now; at the time, I didn't see that I'd fully accepted my role as his dependant. I'd fallen for him and his hair-patting mother.

When the Pirate saw me, he puffed out his cheeks and came across the room to help me inside. He told me to lie down on a long bench at the back of the taverna.

'Eat,' he said.

'I can't. I'll throw up.'

'I know what to give you.'

As I lay on the bench seat, I enjoyed the coolness of its synthetic cushioning on my face. From under the tables, I could see the Pirate's mum walking around the restaurant hurriedly. I slept for a bit.

When I woke, the Pirate's mum was walking towards me. She sat down and stroked my hair. Usually, it made me feel odd, appropriated into a wish for a girl companion, but now it was comforting, as though she might know what to do to help me. She made me sit up and smiled. A pirate's mother telling me it would be alright.

'Drink, drink,' she said. She had brought me a bowl of soup, made of fish head and tomato.

'I'm sorry, I can't.'

'Yes, drink it.'

I'd hardly ever heard her speak English. But maybe the word *drink* was one she'd heard often in the Pirate's taverna, if it really was his. Suddenly, I questioned even that. Maybe it was her business, and he only worked there when he wasn't pirating. Who knew anything anymore?

The Pirate joined us as though to drive away such imaginings. He gave me a concerned smile. 'Next, bread. And then some wine,' he said.

Wine. The thought of it made me want to vomit. But I ate

what I could of the soup, sipped some water and spent the rest of the morning half asleep on the bench. I saw that he was being very good to me and showing a different side of what it meant to be one of his boys. One other thing the Pirate's mask went some way to conceal – his kindness.

By mid-afternoon, I was coming good. I was able to sit up and keep food and drink down. I relinquished my darker thoughts of night and morning. It was just food poisoning. Europe was alright. The trip was worth it. It was right to travel with an open mind and heart.

I sipped the Pirate's wine and watched two local men arrive for their afternoon drinks or coffee, talking quietly about their day. I thought some more about my trip, and reminded myself I was glad I'd come. It had been necessary to meet my father and accept the comforts of this island refuge for a while after. But it was time to find my way out. I believe they were my first proper steps out of childhood.

Paul arrived at the taverna late in the afternoon. 'What happened to you?' he asked chirpily. 'You look terrible.'

'Bad cheese,' I said. I wasn't in the mood for banter. 'Where have you been?'

'Me and Felix headed out. I met a girl.' After a pause, he added, 'I think I'm in love.'

'You were having sex while I was dying?'

'There's no need to be like that.'

'We have to get out of here,' I said.

'Nice idea. But no cash, my friend.'

I corrected him about that. 'We've got the money in the wallet.'

Paul grimaced. 'Not quite.'

'You spent it all?'

'I may have. Give it another week. We'll get some work and go.'

'I'm leaving tomorrow,' I insisted. 'You can come or stay. It's up to you.'

Paul turned away, scowling. 'One day, you'll listen to me. I told you. We've got no money!'

I was furious that he'd spent everything in the wallet. It meant that I'd have to find a way to pay for us both to get back to Scotland. But it was unfair to judge him too harshly, as we'd never been sensible about money. Why would that have changed now, when he was out late having a good time? As it was, I still had enough drachmas left over from the night before to get a bus to Corfu Town, and we already had our ferry tickets to Athens. I just needed Paul to come round to the idea of leaving tomorrow.

I watched the Pirate ready the taverna for the night ahead. Probably, it would be quiet tonight, and he wouldn't have to work too hard. He was so many things: a host, a reveller, a cook; kind and nostalgic, violent, sexist and foul-mouthed, accepting. On the best days, he offered friendship; on the worst, he was terrifying. And so, despite the care he'd shown me, I believed his plans to cross the oceans for purposes that were probably half legal or worse. I believed his threat that he'd throw us overboard if we didn't get along with the crew.

I also worried that he wouldn't let me leave.

Felix came in and joined me and Paul at the table. He was going to sail to Brazil, no matter what. He thought we should, too. I'd made up my mind that it was time to flee, but I didn't want Felix to know. Our debt to the Pirate now stood at eight thousand drachmas: eighty dollars, too much to pay through a last job that might come our way. We were going to have to make an escape with that amount unpaid.

So, to Felix, I said we weren't sure yet. To Paul, later that night at the villa, I said it had to be in the morning. 'Otherwise, we're stuck here for the winter. If we get to Athens, we can scrounge enough for tickets to London. Or I'll use Mum's credit card.' It was the last thing I wanted to do; she could hardly afford to help us. But it was coming to that.

'What about the Pirate?' Paul asked. 'What about the money?'

'We can't pay him, can we?'

'Aye, we can. Another week. There'll be work.'

'Paul, the season's over. We have to go.'

He went to his room again, as angry with me as the last time we talked about it. I sat down on my bed and read, thinking there was going to have to be another row. I wasn't going to leave him here. Neither of us wanted that, not really. But an hour or so later, he walked down the corridor and said, 'I thought there was a chance we could stay on.'

'Where's the girl you met staying?' I asked. She was on his mind, I could tell.

'I don't really know. She's probably left already.'

'We'll get the bus tomorrow. The first one, before he's up.'

'How will we pay him?'

'We'll send the money from home. Seven-thirty: the early bus. Before he knows we're gone. Before he's up. It has to be that bus.'

'He'll kill us if he sees us.'

'I know.'

For the first time since we'd arrived at the villa, we cleaned up; I'd had a go at the vomit already. If we were going to do a

160

runner, we would at least leave things looking nice. We swept dust into plastic bags and tidied away the last items that might suggest that anyone had lived in the half-finished villa: a few books, a dozen empty bottles, bed linen washed by hand.

A note, too. Wasn't that what you should do? A note to say that we'd send the Pirate the money as soon as we could, from Glasgow or Brisbane. This is what I wrote to him.

Dear Pirate,

We won't ever be able to pay the money we owe you if we stay. We think it's best to head back to London and send you the money from there. Thank you for everything you've done for us. I know we'll see you again one day.

Your friends, Kári and Paul

Such was the first debt that I would take with me from that time. A promise to pay the Pirate. I hated the note, and I hated what we were doing. What would you call it? A cowardly exit. Deceit. Theft, even. Piracy! Much more than just not paying a bill, for the Pirate was so much more than that kind of host; he didn't even believe in bills. For all that, I left the note on the kitchen bench underneath the corner of an ashtray and hoped he would understand.

Just before seven the next morning, we walked out into the wind and up towards the village. It was still dim between the farmhouses and fenced gardens and goat pens; the dogs didn't stir. We reached the crest in the lane and the main road, and the bench in front of the taverna, where the bus stopped.

The morning bus service would save us, return us to Corfu Town, a ferry to Athens. I'd almost certainly have to use Mum's credit card to buy us tickets to London. And then, when things were normal again, I'd write to him with the money. It wouldn't be a problem. Eighty dollars. Such a payable amount, if only you could pay it from there rather than from here.

We sat down on the bench and waited. Across the street, a group of girls emerged from the houses. The ones we'd seen before. They glanced at us over each other's shoulders. Then a bus came. I thought it was our bus, but no.

'Athens around the corner,' I said.

'Aye.'

'And then you'll be back home.'

'Back to Scotland.'

We heard the window latches of upstairs apartments begin to unlock. Children waking and calling to their parents. The first smell of coffee in the street. I wished the bus would come. Then, a delivery truck. It, too, looked like the front of our bus. But it wasn't.

The sliding door of the taverna began to move and the Pirate's face appeared. 'Boys?' he said. 'You want coffee?'

Oh, no. What was the Pirate doing up this early? 'No, thank you,' I replied.

'What are you doing?' But even as he asked, he saw our backpacks and knew. 'You're going?'

I tried to guess what might be going through his mind. Had we robbed him, made a mess of the villa? Had he been wrong about us all this time? *His boys*. I couldn't tell. His expression was tired.

'We have to go,' I said.

'I see.' He put a foot into the street.

I rushed an explanation. 'We can't stay any longer. There's no work. We've run out of money. We haven't had a job for a week.'

He shook his head. 'There's always work. Come with me to Brazil.'

'No. We should have told you,' I said.

The Pirate stood still beside the door. 'Yes.'

He made no mention of the money, but I had to bring it up. 'We'll never pay you back if we stay. We'll go home and send it to you from there.'

He was still inscrutable behind the fog of his morning exhaustion. He looked awful. But then, he was always like this in the mornings. 'Come here,' he said. We stepped towards him, and he approached us.

'No, closer. Here,' he said, grabbing our shirts.

He put an arm around my shoulder, his other hand reaching behind his back. I watched it. Was there a knife? And then he lifted that hand, and it was as empty and open as before. He put it around Paul's shoulder. Then he hugged and kissed us.

'Boys,' he said. 'Don't you know I love you? You should have trusted me.'

Love?

'You can go,' he said. 'Of course.'

'I'm sorry,' I said.

'I love you, boys,' he repeated.

As he spoke, our bus arrived. We owed eighty dollars to the Pirate, but also any amount one might nominate for being released. He was letting us go if we needed to. With that, we boarded the bus and left the Pirate and the village of Karousades, for now, and I had my second debt – the permission to go.

14

The spaces between us

Corfu, September 2022

Back at the apartment, we nap lightly for the last hour of the afternoon, before choosing somewhere to have dinner. A taverna at the end of a narrow lane that winds down to Yialos beach, also close to Karousades, has good reviews for its traditional Greek food, so we phone them but can't get through, and we can't find anywhere to make an online booking. We decide that Finnur and I might as well make the ten-minute drive to the restaurant to see if we can reserve a table.

Finnur shakes his brother's hair and makes a joke about Magnús staying behind with his mum. 'We'll do it, champ,' he quips. 'You just relax. Rest up.'

Magnús takes the bait and stands up. 'I'll come,' he says indignantly.

'Joke, joke,' Finnur assures him, and Magnús sits down again.

The boys are friends, probably best friends, even if that's not how they'd describe it. Not yet. They criticise each other quite a lot: Magnús gets annoyed by his older brother's bossiness and confidence, and Finnur lambasts his younger brother for being disorganised and not assertive enough. In other words, they find fault in the very qualities they foster in each other.

But at times like this, when it's just me and one of the boys, I'm struck by the loyalty and affection they share. They speak so fondly about one another. Similarly, if ever they've been hurt in sports, or in the tumble of everyday life in a small house with three large males and a dog (Olanda takes up rather less space than we do), they've cared for each other, nagging whoever's been injured to rest and recover, almost to the point of becoming a third parent. The space between them disappears, just like when they steal, or 'borrow', each other's shoes, or a shirt, a bus card, charging cables.

Who knows how much credit a parent can take for this tenderness and care? But their closeness feels like more than just good luck, and Olanda and I have worked hard at getting the boys to respect each other. Our method, if it can be called that, is to be deliberate in our own respect for their views and interests, from music to sport to the things they're most keen on doing when travelling. Perhaps the word for this is *equality* in our relationship with them, but in fact it almost amounts to a kind of submission on our part, a relegating of our identities to theirs, one that I've noticed is similar to an author's submission to a story they're writing. The work is your creation, and to begin with it follows your design. But eventually a story must develop its own momentum, the characters their own agency, and the author allows themselves to follow, to become part of the narrative rather than its determiner. That must be part of the reason it's so hard for parents to step back: the sense of loss is like coming to the end of a story you have loved writing.

*

Finnur is coming up to the point where he has to make his subject selections for the last two years of high school. His English teacher thinks he should take the literature extension course: he's strong in the subject, although for now he likes the creative writing assignments more than the literary analysis.

'I imagine it's a lot of reading,' I say. 'Are you up for that?'

'Yeah,' he answers, unconvincingly. 'It's only four or five books a year.'

'How many have you read this year?'

He smiles but doesn't answer. Before I left for Corfu, I gave him a copy of Durrell's *My Family and Other Animals*, which he's brought with him and has made a good start on. He says it's old-fashioned in its language, but he likes it.

'You could say that book is about openness to the world,' I suggest.

'And dealing with family members,' he replies, with a playful glint in his eyes. The road is tight; a delivery van coming the other way tucks into the low shrubs beside the road and we wave our thanks. He goes one, 'My other subjects will be regular English, economics, modern history, biology and maths.'

They're the exact same subjects I did for my Senior, but I don't mention it; Finnur's a bit too used to being told he's like me, and I can't imagine he wants to hear it now, when he's planning his own future. 'Good choices,' I say. 'Not drama, though?' He's been doing very well in that subject, too.

'Nah,' he says. 'Well, maybe. But I don't think so. I can still be in the play if I want to.' As I was, even though I didn't do the subject either.

Let him make his own decisions, I remind myself, while he replicates the steps I took at school. It's only the latest iteration of the uncanny similarities between us. His early physical likeness to me was so striking that people wondered out loud whether Olanda had been involved at all, and we hadn't simply had some kind of clone made. As he reached his teens, he could even open my phone using the face ID. Now that he's arrived at the close of true boyhood, his face has changed – it's lengthened and become more angular and masculine, and some of the likeness has faded. I remember the day the face recognition software declined him entry into my phone. 'Damn,' he said, 'I'll have to start typing your password.'

Olanda says we have exactly the same temperament, too. I suppose it's harder for me to recognise that. In him, I see quite a strong, perhaps over-confident personality – a classic older brother. We argue much more than Magnús and I do, which is allegedly a sign of similarity. Even if I disagree with Magnús or he's annoyed with me, we almost never raise our voices. Finnur and I can shout at one another for ten minutes, and an hour later we've more or less forgotten whatever it was that had us so worked up.

It feels like the right moment to ask him. 'What do you think of the runner we did?'

'Wasn't great.'

'Why?'

'You didn't trust someone who helped you. I get why you did it, though. You were desperate to get out of there. But sometimes you've got to face up to what you've done, right? That's what you're always telling us. Take responsibility.'

'Yes. I should have faced it then and there and didn't.'

'It's lucky we can come back,' he says. *We.*

'Thank the Pirate together.'

We find the Yialos taverna's driveway on the left side of the road, just before we get to the end and the beach access. I turn into the car park. The taverna is shut, but next to the patio there's a house; I tell Finnur it's likely to be where the owners live. 'Can you see if they'll give us a table?'

'Why me?'

'I don't feel like having to,' I say.

'Nor do I, though. You're the Greek expert, you do it.'

'I'm not a Greek expert. You already know as much about the place as I do. Go on. It'll be good for your confidence.'

'But you're always telling me I'm too confident. *Cocky*, I've heard you say.'

And on it goes for a while, until finally Finnur gives in and agrees to knock on the door of the house to find out whether we can make a booking.

When Finnur and I get back, we all take it in turns to have a shower. The hot water system for the apartment comes with stern warnings about how to get the right temperature without causing harm and destruction to oneself and the hot water system itself. You have to turn it on thirty minutes before you want a shower, and then turn if off while you're having the shower. The reward for this exactitude is a hostile jet spray inside one of those 1980s blue-tiled cubicles. The hand-held shower head coats the entire bathroom in water. I hear Magnús laughing as it happens now and can only imagine the state of the walls and the floor.

I wait on the balcony, watching the last of the direct sunlight in the valley. Eventually, the light seems to be inside the hills and stone walls of the villages: the boundary between the light and the landscape disappears, revealing how everything dissolves into its beginnings.

I remember a conversation with a colleague about boundaries in parenting. She told me that she'd recently had to remind her daughter that they *weren't* friends. She wanted her daughter to know that she would always help her and provide advice and support. But that was quite different from friendship, which to my colleague suggested a relationship of equals. Being a parent was not about being your child's equal, she told me, because children need to know that you have the final say, and the responsibility.

I was a little shocked to hear it. Yes, I felt responsible for the boys, and naturally we had to set some rules. But the idea that I was superior to my children hadn't occurred to me. More surprising still was how much my colleague had developed an *approach* to parenting. I realised I didn't even have much of a view of what we were doing, let alone an entire approach.

She must have seen my thoughts in my expression. 'Well, what did you think you were doing when you had kids?' she asked. 'Creating a new group of friends?'

Yes, I reflected. That, and more. And so, now I'm the one who needs the lessons in boundaries and space.

Later, at dinner at the taverna, Finnur reports on the trauma of the table booking. After he agreed to go in, he knocked on the door of the house and it swung open by itself. I watched him pop his head behind the doorway and call out hello, and then step inside.

When he came back to the car, he wasn't sure whether we had a booking. *What do you mean, you're not sure?* I'd asked, before hearing a version of the story he's telling now.

'There were about eight guys sitting at a table, looking *really* serious,' Finnur says. 'And an old lady. She looked really serious, as well. It was like walking in on some mafia meeting.'

'I think you might be exaggerating a little,' I say, which is also what I told him in the car.

'Nah. I was about to get dragged in and stabbed. Definitely only just got away with my life.'

Magnús joins in. 'You've been listening to too many of Dad's stories. Not everyone's a pirate, you know.'

Magnús glances in my direction, and I see again his ability to maintain a generosity and openness, a viewpoint that I also try to adopt. But, though a shared trait, Magnús also surprises me with how easily he manages to do things on his own. If we're somewhere new, he'll quite happily look up the bus routes and head off to the shops or nearest sports fields by himself, asking to join in a game of basketball if there's one going. We always offer him a lift, but often he declines, preferring to make his own discoveries, even if it might mean getting lost. I read this as his way of inhabiting places by having to learn them physically: a form of spatial thinking that I also loved when I was a boy, when I would spend hours tracing the streets of Reykjavík by foot or on my bike. A form of thinking that was also part of what brought me to Corfu when I was eighteen.

'You didn't see them!' says Finnur, defending his account of what he witnessed. 'They were scary.'

In my mind's eye, I see a mother and her sons, perhaps some of the restaurant workers, having a meeting about the dinner they're preparing for that night. But who's to say? Maybe Finnur escaped a kidnapping, and we're lucky to have him back.

Regardless, we decided to risk it, and have been received with nothing but smiles and hospitality. Finnur riffs on his encounter, and during the meal he attempts to convince us that the taverna is a front for a syndicate of pirates. What he saw earlier in the day, when he was on his own in the house, that was the real thing. The beautiful patio and Greek feast; a friendly waitress who appears with our orders; the music and the sound of the waves: all part of the act.

'Sure,' I say. But his elaborate theory brings the conversation back to *my* pirate, and whether Paul and I were really in any danger when we planned our runner and got caught at the bus stop.

'Did you think he was actually going to be violent?' Magnús asks.

'It was the pig slaughter that did it,' I say. 'He was so capable.'

'But how else are you meant to kill a pig?'

It's a fair point. 'I always had a bit of an imagination,' I concede. 'Probably, it was all in my head.'

Magnús shoots a look of faux surprise at Finnur. 'Sound familiar?'

Finnur whispers, 'Just you wait. In a minute the lights will go out, and we'll be ordered into a van, and taken for ransom.'

'It's a shame we're not worth very much,' Olanda jokes. Then, 'The bit I'm wondering about is not whether he was going to kill you and Paul but whether he meant it when he said *he* was hurt, when he said he loved you. He really was that close to you?'

Over the years, I've also wondered about those parting words of the Pirate. There was fondness on his part, I'm sure. But, on reflection, perhaps what mattered as much to him was that we recognise that his wish to help us, and others like us, was genuine. His love was the openness he showed strangers, and the joy he took in welcoming them. We had lost sight of that.

15

The Pirate's business card

After we left Corfu, Paul and I made a slightly disgruntled, mainly relieved journey to Glasgow, one that was much quicker than our travels to Athens. We spent a night sleeping in a park on the esplanade in Corfu Town, waiting for a ferry to mainland Greece the next day. There, I used Mum's credit card to pay for a sixty-hour coach ride from Athens to London, the route crossing Bulgaria, Yugoslavia, and then Austria, Germany and France. We were as broke as we'd been when we left Brindisi, but this time, instead of a carton of cigarettes, we bought six bottles of drinking water, thinking there wouldn't be any on the way. The water was fine, but we didn't eat until we got to London with five full bottles of Evian.

I wasn't destitute: I did have Mum's credit card, even if I hated using it, and we were able to stay with friends that night in London. Also, before I'd left Aviemore, Mum had sent me a seven-day BritRail Pass for my birthday present. It allowed you any seven days' travel within a three-month period, including overnight trips. The pass covered my trip to Glasgow, where I had to collect my suitcase from Paul's place, but I had to use the credit card again to buy him a ticket.

I thought I might be able to sleep at Paul's house for a few nights but, when we got to Glasgow, his mum said she couldn't have me to stay, not if I was broke. She could barely afford to feed herself and Paulie, let alone a boarder.

She cooked us a late lunch of eggs and chips and white bread with strong tea, and then I fetched my suitcase from under the stairs and got ready to go. Paul and I had been travelling together for nearly three months; it was seven months since we'd met. I hadn't stopped liking him, but I don't think either of us was sad to say goodbye.

'Where are you going to go?' he asked.

'Edinburgh,' I said.

'Jessica?' he asked, surprised. In London, we'd heard that she was still with her old boyfriend in Edinburgh, the one she'd gone back to when she sensed that I wasn't going to stay in Aviemore. 'What about the other fella?' Paul said.

'I'm not trying to start anything,' I said. 'I just want to say goodbye properly, that's all.'

We hugged a few times and said we'd stay in touch, but I'm sure we both knew that our friendship had run its course. I haven't seen him since, and I haven't been able to find him while writing this book. We'd helped each other to follow the road, and now it was time to accept that we'd misunderstood what its freedoms meant.

'Will you go and see your daughter tonight?' I asked him.

'Aye, I called Leah just now, while you were fighting under the stairs with that beast from the depths.'

'The wee one's alright?'

'Bouncing bonny lass,' said Paul, quoting Leah, I thought. 'She knows I'll be over later.'

'Our Paulie's a da,' I said, quoting Leah as well.

'Aye, he is that.'

It was early December and bitterly cold. The next day, Paul found me fifteen pounds, part-payment for his tickets. Though it wasn't much, at least I had some cash. I had nine nights to fill before a flight would carry me back to Brisbane. I boarded an afternoon train to Edinburgh, grateful to be alone again. The afternoon was a bright one, the Scottish lowlands softened by thinning winter light and the blurring speed of the train.

I arrived in Edinburgh just before four, found the apartment where Jessica lived with her boyfriend, and knocked on the door. No answer. I waited and tried again, but the same. I had no idea what to do next. Get on the night train back to London? I stepped back into the street and found a bench next to a garden with high, black-painted iron gates. I decided to let it go: there was a time for saying goodbye but also a time for moving on. I was about to stand up and pull my suitcase to the train station when she walked around the corner.

Jessica said she couldn't have me to stay with her in Edinburgh; apparently, her boyfriend didn't like me very much. But she owned a small apartment in Kirkcaldy, only half an hour away by train, and I could have the place for the week, if I could get by on having little more than a bed. She organised for a key to be left under a winter-bare pot plant by the front door and, after we said goodbye, I left to stay there, and began the long wait for the day of my flight.

It was viciously cold inside, even colder than outside. As Jessica had warned, there was a bed but that was it. No covers or blankets. I pulled down the curtains for a bedspread and tipped all my clothes out of my suitcase. I wore everything I could, including a jumper and scarf and gloves. It was a rather undignified end to my gap year. But soon I'd be home, warm and well fed. I would start university and get a job and post the money that I owed the Pirate.

Or, as it turned out, not post it. There was no proper reason for not doing so. Once I got back on my feet in Brisbane, I had the money – it was a relatively small amount, after all. I should have put it in an envelope, posted it and paid my debt, and that would have brought the Corfu chapter of my life to a well-balanced close. But perhaps I didn't want that to happen. Maybe the hint of danger, or of uncertainty at least, was more satisfying than a resolution. It was a way of keeping the island with me, a magical spell that promised a return.

I sensed that this feeling – one of wanting things to be both stable and uncertain, settled and unpredictable – was one that the boys understood from their youngest years. When they were little, their favourite games all involved me lifting them in one way or another. We called one Roller Coaster, in which they would sit on my knees while the roller coaster (my legs) clunked up to the top of the ride. As we climbed higher, we'd point out birds, planes and tall buildings, and marvel at how small all the people on the ground were. At the top, the ride would slow, my knees would drop, and then we'd swirl up and down and sideways to the bottom again, the boys screaming with glee.

If we were out and the boys were tired and wanted a ride on my shoulders, they had recourse to a special button on my left arm, a faded mole near my wrist that they pressed to activate a lift. The button dinged, my hands swung down, and up they went, lifted skywards into the infinity of the sky at the same as they landed on the sureness of my shoulders.

I came to learn that this combination of danger and security featured in all of the boys' favourite adventures. I could see the tingling sensation of risk in their eyes, such as one day when we were at the zoo and a goat that was behind Finnur jumped onto a fence. When he turned around to see what the noise was, he and the goat were face to face, each as shocked as the other. We burst out laughing, and so did he – with the pure incongruity of the moment, the goat's cheekiness and our delight at how things so suddenly were turned upside down.

Sometimes, it felt as if my own life had been turned upside down and tossed in a different ocean, where the only pirates were the boys playing with toy ships and plastic cannons in the bath. Bath time was heaven sent, for no matter how annoyed the boys might be with each other, once they got in the water their moods changed and they collaborated on military campaigns that were immediately underway. After they got out, we lined up their toys on the carpet in their bedroom and arranged new battles with hot rod cars, Lego castles, spitfires, Vikings and carriages from *Thomas the Tank Engine* – the Fat Controller and Miss Jane on different sides of skirmishes that ended in the crashing and piling of battalions – and then quiet time, a story to end the day.

I did a good Ringo Starr impersonation. He was the first narrator of *Thomas the Tank Engine,* and listening to his voice on DVD reissues brought back memories of watching the show in England when I was a boy – in the long summer holidays, when I'd watch anything. 'Magnús had a special,' I intoned in my best Liverpudlian accent. 'The children at the beach had run out of ice-cream. *You'll have to go straight away*, said Miss Jane. *It's so hot! The children will be waiting!* Toot, toot!'

Was there anything of the Pirate left in me? No, of course not. Or not unless pirates could also be men entering middle age who at night struggled to keep their eyes open long enough to tell a bedtime story. Some of these involved my own perilous adventures when I was their age; I marvelled at how they didn't tire of hearing these tales over and over again.

But I learnt that children have a particular way of listening that seems to allow the humour and poignancy of the past to co-exist, not only harmoniously but as complementary perspectives. The boys were attentive and contemplative listeners, and open to the play of story elements, which they didn't seem to want to iron out or reconcile. I told them a silly tale about how, when I lived in Iceland as a boy, my friends and I used to leave our morning swimming classes with our hair still wet, so it would freeze and we could snap it. Another was about the ice tunnels we used to make in snow mounds formed by ploughs clearing the roads, until the local council saw what we were doing and collapsed the tunnels before we managed to get ourselves buried by snow.

Each of these stories featured the truant perspective of a lone child brought up in a single-parent family. I was quite sure they understood that, and gently folded an awareness of my playful loneliness as a child into their enjoyment of the freedom I had. Fatherhood allowed experiences like these to be shared in a way that found the mirth and adventure of the past as a story world, a palace of rooms filled with gems that the boys also claimed as their own. Like the readers of a book, they took possession of the stories and shaped them towards their own interests.

*

Once, when we were on a family holiday at Phú Quốc Island in Vietnam, we took a boat ride to visit some smaller islands nearby, to picnic and snorkel. It was just the four of us and a young captain on a tiny vessel with an enormous engine that looked as though it had been extracted from a tractor. On our way back, the captain began to steer the boat in circles that got tighter and tighter, the boat tipping and swaying, spray from the engine and sides covering us in water.

The boys screamed, holding each other and us, in disbelief at this unexpected change. They were scared out of their wits and also howling with laughter. Just like when the goat appeared on the fence, it was so much fun to see how the world could be turned on its head, out of nowhere.

We talked about the boat ride for days afterwards, their accounts of it changing from the fear they'd felt to declarations that it wasn't that bad, and then to when could we go again. Wasn't there another free day for a second boat ride? 'Can't we go back?' they asked, over and over.

'We're visiting the pepper farm and squid-sauce refinery next,' I reminded them, but these attractions didn't seem to hold the same appeal.

'Let's go back to the island,' they insisted.

That's how I felt about the Pirate, too. The further I got from that wild year, the more I wanted a little of it back, appreciating it more and more as time eased away the troubles of those months and left only the finer impressions of the jewel-like Corfu and its long nights and slow meals. Their glow. I didn't pretend that I could be my eighteen-year-old self again. I had no great wish to be desperate and hungry and broke. But I sensed something left in my debt to the Pirate, a story that needed a better ending. A coda that existed alongside not only my gratitude to the Pirate, but also my gratitude for where I was in my life now. Fatherhood was what I'd been waiting for my whole adult life: I saw it as my main job and what I most wanted to get right. Even if I couldn't quite place it perfectly yet, I was sure the moment the Pirate let me go was part of what had led me to that realisation.

A full twenty years had passed, and I still owed eighty dollars in Corfu. Yes, I know, scandalous. After all that time, I hadn't paid the Pirate. I had broken my promise to him, despite everything he did for me and Paul. Still, it no longer seemed right to simply post the money, as I now saw that the debt was more than a financial one.

It was 2010, the year of my father's death. His passing brought with it a strange grief, one that I almost felt I wasn't entitled to, as I'd never truly known him. How could I grieve someone who wasn't really mine? But his death did alter the nature of his absence, from one that might be mended to one that could only be given life in stories and memories that others had of him.

That grief somehow also came to be folded into a feeling that I needed to do more in the matter of the Pirate, perhaps because the same sense of loss had accompanied our first meeting, when I'd left the meeting with my father in Reykjavík and ended up at Corfu Town. I began looking for the Pirate online. I didn't know his actual name: all I could do was google 'Pirate', 'taverna' and 'Karousades' and see what came up. Nothing. It was as though he'd never existed, at least not in that guise. Or he'd disappeared to his other life in Brazil, or perhaps even to the next life altogether. How long did taverna-owning pirates live?

Another year passed.

Then, one day, the past shot up in an even more demanding way.

In a cupboard in my study, I had a stack of boxes that I never opened. Olanda and I had decided to sort out the cupboard and put things into proper containers to keep out the ants that sometimes marched into the study from the forest at the back of our house.

We bought three big plastic containers from the hardware store and began transferring things. Soon, I was distracted by all the keepsakes I'd long forgotten I had. Olanda said we'd have a better chance of getting the job done if we didn't stop to peruse every one of them, but I couldn't help it. It was so enjoyable to see the objects that emerged, as though from the deep ocean: photos from Iceland and Scotland, including one of me and Paul in a car park in Aviemore, climbing a massive, long-discarded playground dinosaur that was stored outside the staff hostel.

'Let me work on the other boxes while you keep going on that one,' Olanda eventually said, losing faith in my ability to focus on the job at hand.

'Don't you want to see all my old junk?'

'It's fascinating but, you know, we still have a lot to clear out.'

'Yes, you're right,' I said. 'Hang on, what's this?' At the bottom of the box was an old leather shoulder bag I'd had at university.

'I think I'll make us a cup of tea,' Olanda said, giving up completely.

I'd already started opening the bag. 'That sounds nice.'

'So that you can look through this and then we can get back to it.'

'Exactly.'

Inside the leather bag were three items from the year that

I went to see my father and met the Pirate. The Karousades Camping brochure Helena gave us as we stepped off the ferry. A calendar I'd drawn up with all the travel dates for the journey to Athens; it also tracked in detail our declining cash balance.

But then smallest, and most buried of all, a business card with an address written in Greek. It must be the Pirate's, I thought, but I had no recollection of being given it. I could only guess that he'd given it to me so that I had an address to mail the eighty dollars. The first pieces of a story that I must have known that one day I would want to resume. 'You won't believe what's in the bag,' I exclaimed.

'Kettle's on,' Olanda called back. 'Can't hear you.'

I joined her in the kitchen and showed her the business card. 'Can you read it?' she asked.

'I can't read any Greek,' I said. 'But look on the back. He wrote a name. Elisseos. I think it must be *his* name. It's the Pirate!'

Olanda read my thoughts. 'Oh god, you want to go and see him now, don't you?' she said. 'You think he's alive.'

'I doubt it,' I said. 'But he probably wasn't all that old. Our age now or even younger. If he's in his sixties, he could still be going.'

'Pirating,' Olanda said. She took her tea into the living room and sat on the couch.

'Aren't we going to keep going?' I asked.

'You still want to? I thought you'd be off looking up the Pirate now that you've got his card!'

'Actually, yes, I'd prefer to do that.'

'Show me what you find,' she said, and took a sip of her tea.

I sat at my laptop in the study and googled 'Elisseos' and 'Karousades'. Still nothing. Then I tried 'Elisseos Corfu taverna'. Though there were hundreds of tavernas in Corfu, not one of the search results came up with the Pirate's dark eyes and long black hair, not even his hospitable side – when he smiled and held his arms wide open, a glass of his rosé in hand.

Olanda came back in and I showed her the pictures of Karousades I'd found, and others of the bays in the north of the island. I clicked my way from pirates and tavernas to Kalami, the village where the Durrells spent some of their time in the 1930s when they lived in Corfu.

'How beautiful,' Olanda said. 'Is the water really that clear?'

'It is. Where *the blue really begins*,' I added, quoting the Lawrence Durrell phrase I loved so much. 'That's exactly how it is. I felt like I hadn't ever really seen clear blue water before.'

'But this is Kalami, not Karousades?'

'Karousades is inland, in the hills,' I said. 'Less pretty as well. No, that's not right. Pretty in a different way. Not luxurious.' I closed the laptop.

The boys, who were five and three at the time, came in and asked what we were doing. 'Do you want to see something?' I asked.

'Sure,' said Finnur.

I reached for one of the boxes that held old photos and pulled out a red album with pictures from the year I met the Pirate. The boys leant close to me, one against each arm, as I flicked through the first pages and saw a photo of the night we ate with the Swedish couple Vidar and Elsa.

Finnur put his fingertip on an orange smudge in the corner of the photo. 'I think I remember what happened,' I said. 'The person taking the picture – his name was Chrisos – kept putting a finger in front of the lens. I'm pretty sure I called across the room and asked him to move it, but it looks like he didn't move it enough. The blur is from his finger.'

'Is that really you, Dad?' asked Finnur.

'It is.'

'Your hair is so long!'

'Still me, though,' I said. 'I was eighteen.'

'Who else is in the picture?' he asked, as though that might help solve the mystery of how differently I appeared.

'That's my friend Paul,' I said, pointing at the other young man at the front of the table. 'And there's Felix. He was a soldier from Austria. The older people are a couple from Sweden who we had dinner with that night. And the man who you can't see all of, well, we called him the Pirate.'

That afternoon, for the first time, I told them the Pirate story, in its broadest strokes. How we'd met him, a *real* pirate, and how he helped us to get back on our feet, and then we did a runner. 'I still owe him the money,' I concluded, and felt the hollowness of a poor ending, especially now that it was a story for my sons. There was a quality of *getting away with it* to the tale, but that wasn't what we wanted the story to be.

'Will you pay him?' asked Finnur later that night, at dinner. He'd been thinking it over, too.

'I should,' I said. 'It's a bit of a disgrace that I haven't done so before.'

'*Disgrace*, Dad,' said Magnús, repeating the word without really understanding it.

With that, Finnur and Magnús became part of the project of paying the Pirate, which of course also meant discovering what the true, fuller nature of the debt might be. I have learnt that I've needed their help with that part of the story, as well.

*

That summer, as we came into 2012, I began to sketch out the possibility of a return trip to Corfu. I didn't know what I would find, but the story was alive again in my life, and in the shared life of my family. As I couldn't find the Pirate online, I'd pay him back in person; it was the only way.

Olanda wasn't as sure about me going back to Corfu. 'What if he's got a grudge against you?' she asked. 'I mean, you haven't paid him for twenty years. He might be angry. Violent!'

'It's a long time ago,' I said.

'Exactly. No-one would expect you to pay an eighty-dollar bill from when you were eighteen. Why's it so important?'

'I'm not exactly sure. But don't you think we all have something like this in our past: a time we didn't get it right? When we were young and stupid and left without ... I don't know, the right goodbye.'

'We don't all go back to fix it. Especially not to a pirate.'

'That's just what he called himself.'

'Then why did you get so scared and make a getaway?'

'Well, I guess we *were* a bit scared. I didn't want to end up a pirate, for starters.'

'Who knows, you might end up one now,' she answered, giggling to herself. 'A mid-life pirate instead of a mid-life crisis.'

There was a monetary debt that ought to have been paid. There was more to it than that, I knew, but for the moment that was all I could really say with certainty. That was enough for now. I bought a ticket to Greece. Then, delays. Mum fell ill a few days before I was meant to fly to Athens, and I postponed my travels. But another two years on, I had the opportunity I needed. I was travelling to Europe for a conference in London; I added a weekend side trip to Corfu.

So much time had passed; it was now nearing twenty-five years since I'd lived in Karousades. It seemed very unlikely that I would find the Pirate, or that he would remember me if I did.

I printed the photograph of me with him and Paul and Felix and the Swedish tourists toasting the evening meal they were about to pay for, Chrisos's photo, as a memory prompt for the Pirate, should it be needed. And, with that, I began a trip back to Corfu to pay him his eighty dollars, and to offer my thanks, if he was still where I'd left him all that time ago.

16

Eighty dollars

Corfu, September 2014

Whenever I've spoken to others about the decision to return to Corfu twenty-four years after I incurred the debt to the Pirate, they've often found it quite odd; as I said, I myself didn't fully understand it at the time. But the necessity of returning felt very strong, and for the time being I elected to trust that feeling and let it be my guide.

As my flight descended into Corfu, the streets below looked empty and quiet. My breath quickened: I was desperate to get off the plane, as anxious to be out of the airport as the happy English tourists around me, here to catch the last of summer. They talked about going straight to the beach in the morning. When the seatbelt sign was off, the young man sitting next to me sighed and said, 'You're not one of those people who push their way out, are you?'

Not usually. But that night, I wouldn't have minded if he let me out, even if we all ended up together again at the baggage carousel. 'No hurry,' I lied, and smiled.

'So pointless,' he said.

'They're just pleased to be here, I expect.'

But then a woman standing in the line paused to let us get up. 'I suppose it's our turn after all,' the young man concluded.

All flight, I'd been almost too tired to keep my eyes open, still jetlagged from the flight to London a few days before. Now, I was wide awake. At the top of the plane stairs, the air smelt of tarmac and fuel, mixed with the stewards' perfume and aftershave. But behind that was the ocean and stone walls of villages and the dusty hills of olive groves.

I collected my suitcase and found a taxi. I'd already booked a room at Hotel Atlantis. It was a little scruffy and dated in the pictures online, but I liked its location next to the port.

'You want Atlantis?' my driver said, sounding surprised.

'Near the port, right?' I said.

'That is Hotel Atlantis,' he answered.

We took the first streets in silence. The windows of the taxi were open, and gradually the feeling of the night changed from the yard-like silences near the airport to the tightness of the old town. At the corners, the headlights brightened walls of yellow and pink and white houses, like stage lights swept across a theatre backdrop.

'First time Corfu?' the driver asked.

'Second.'

'Oh?'

'Yes, second time, but it's more than twenty years between visits.'

'About time, then,' he said, and laughed a smoker's laugh. A packet of cigarettes next to the gear stick was half open. 'Would you like one?' he asked.

'No, thank you.'

'Do you mind?'

'Not at all, go ahead.'

'Not everyone likes it these days,' he mused. He drew on his cigarette and blew the smoke out of the side of his mouth so that it went in a more direct line out the window. A little bit stayed inside.

'Why back, then?' he asked.

'I've wanted to come back for years. I just haven't managed it.'

'You have work here?'

'No.'

'Married?'

'Yes.'

'Kids?'

'Yes. Two boys.'

'Job?'

'Lecturer at a university.'

'Good money?'

'Um, not bad. Fine.'

The rapid-fire interrogation made it feel like my answers weren't adding up for him. I lifted my shoulder bag from beside my feet and took out my wallet, and from inside I retrieved the Pirate's business card that I'd found a couple of years before. I handed it to him.

'Elisseos?' he said as he read it.

'He used to own a taverna in Karousades. He was my friend. I've come back to see if he's still there.' I didn't say, *to see if he's still alive so that I can give him eighty dollars*. There was no reason to imagine that he knew Elisseos, but I couldn't resist: 'Have you met him?'

'I'm from the south,' he said. 'I don't know the people in that village.'

We reached the town esplanade. The street was wider, the frontages of the buildings grand; the dark water of the harbour glistened like an oil spill. Some of the town's ruins, the old Venetian fort, appeared to be crumbling down the main headland, but a thick stone wall built down to the sea was still strong, the skirting defences of a town.

'We never called my friend Elisseos. Only ever the Pirate,' I said.

'Pirate?'

'He was a sailor before he opened a taverna. And he looked like a pirate. A black moustache and long black hair. There was even a drawing of him holding a sword and wearing an eye patch hanging on the wall of his taverna, next to empty bottles that he had on shelves.'

The driver laughed, as though I was exaggerating. The same thing had happened in Brisbane when I described my upcoming trip to our friends. They thought I was beginning a fiction.

'Hotel Atlantis is on the water, near the terminal,' my driver said, not yet reconciled to me staying there. 'People sleep there if they're getting an early ferry.'

'Oh?'

'A bit old, you know.'

'I see,' I said without disappointment. I like old hotels.

'Want a better place? I can do that.'

It was the middle of the night. All I wanted was to get my room key and feel still and be sure this was indeed, as I'd claimed to friends, more real than a fiction, more than a memory. To feel back. 'I like it near the water,' I said, as a sort of explanation.

The driver tapped ash out of the window. 'You choose,' he said. 'And you will find this Elisseos, you think?'

'I hope so.'

The road cut upwards into town and then popped out again at the port. The driver slowed and pulled up to a long rectangular building with a 1960s facade of panels, shutters and slim balconies – quite lovely and entirely of the time when it was built. It looked light, even elegant; old, as well, as my driver had been at pains to say. We stepped out and I took my bag from the boot. It was the beginning of autumn, but still as hot as a tropical night. On the other side of the street, the harbour was a jangly chorus of marina noises: sail ropes against masts, purring generators, trucks reverse-beeping.

'I like it,' I said.

The driver raised his eyebrows and smiled, accepted a tip. 'I hope you find your friend,' he said. 'There are a lot of tavernas in Corfu.'

The hotel's reception desk was dark wood and almost too high for the receptionist to see over as she sat going through paperwork. She pushed her glasses to the bridge of her nose and regarded me for a moment, as though she was a little surprised I was there.

'You are welcome,' she said when I put my case down. 'Reservation?'

'Yes.' I handed her my passport.

'Do you Mr ...' She strained to read my passport. '... *Geeslason* want a room facing the sea?' There was a smile at the corner of her lips, I think because she knew she was miles off with the pronunciation of my name.

'Yes,' I said, 'very much.'

She handed me a small key on a large key ring. 'First floor, second door to the left. No smoking in the room. No extra guests.' Then, remembering her job, she added, 'Please.'

Finally, I was in my room and could sit still and rest. 'Here at last, Elisseos,' I said under my breath, but it didn't sound right, so instead I said what I'd said every time I walked up to the taverna and opened the glass door to find him sitting at his table, cigarette lit, the white phone next to the ashtray, a Coke if it was before lunch, his rosé if it was after. I wouldn't start calling him something else now.

'Hello, Pirate,' I said instead.

I surveyed the room and was pleased I hadn't taken the cab driver's offer of finding somewhere better. The inside was like the outside, in a datedness and austerity that was homely. A hard-mattress bed, one chair tucked under a slim writing table, lamps fastened to the wall. I turned off the air conditioning and opened tall wooden shutters on the windows, which resisted but eventually let in the evening air, along with candle-like spots of orange light, and an envelope of metallic humidity from the harbour. I opened my bag and took out my camera and notebook and moved the desk closer to the window.

My eyes stung from the dry air on the plane. 'A few sentences, at least,' I said to myself. I tried to write up the day, and the sensation of being back in a place that was in my past and now suddenly around me. Freud called it the *uncanny*, a mixture of familiarity and strangeness. But the feeling was also more generous than that. A mixture of relief and electricity, nerves. What was the psychological term for that, I wondered. *Confusion*, perhaps.

I put my notebook away. I couldn't sleep, so I left my room and tiptoed into the corridor. All was silent. Downstairs, the reception was unattended, and I thought it must be too late for a drink, but in the bar was a man on his own, seated in front of a laptop and a half-drunk glass of beer. The young woman at reception was there, too, washing glasses.

She noticed me and waved. 'We're still open, Mr *Geeslason*,' she called.

The other man glanced up for a moment, smiled idly, and returned his gaze to the screen. The sound of scooters and taxis drifted in with a warm breeze. I sat at a table near the front. I thought that maybe I should go back to my room for my laptop, too – write a little more. But it was heavenly just to sit and watch the street and the harbour lights.

'My name is Anastasia,' said the receptionist as she walked from the bar. 'Beer? Ouzo?'

'Beer, thank you,' I said.

'Are you having a good day?'

I smiled and nodded. 'Yeah,' I said. 'Great.'

'You sure? Want me to cheer you up? I tell jokes, you know.' She wore a deadpan expression that was difficult to read. Maybe she did tell jokes. Probably not. 'You like the view?' she asked.

Before I could answer, she left me for the bar, and I heard the fridge opening and the clink of a beer bottle. 'Glass?' she called from behind the bar.

'Please,' I said.

I did like the view, very much. Perhaps it was less appealing if you worked at the hotel every night, but the unpretty roundabout up from the hotel and the noise of the port had a hospitable effect, and also a feeling of busy possibility that somewhere prettier wouldn't have had, because beauty is too much a completed thing, resolved and self-possessed. Corfu Town was still happening.

Anastasia came back with a beer and a glass frosted with cold. I sat at the bar until after one, and then went back to my room and slept soundly in the company of ferry sounds, just as I had on the morning Paul and I sailed in from Brindisi.

I woke at seven and opened the shutters to a morning so bright and clear that it looked like it had been cut into glass. Blue, as always, but also a landscape of mirrors, the port reflected so perfectly in the sea, the Albanian hills a milkier landscape across the strait.

Anastasia was still on reception. 'Don't you get a break?' I asked.

'Don't worry about me,' she said. 'I take all the shifts I can.'

'You didn't ever tell me a joke.'

'Maybe tomorrow,' she said, knowing I wouldn't be here. A corkboard in the hallway was empty but for two leaflets with ferry and bus information, both blurry photocopies with indecipherably complex tables. I felt Anastasia watching me struggling to make sense of it all. 'Where do you want to go?' she asked.

'Karousades.'

'Today? You know it's Sunday, right?' She joined me at the board, put her finger on the paper and traced the times until she found it. 'There's only one bus today,' she said. She tapped the time: ten-fifteen. 'You have to catch that one.'

What was it about Corfu, I wondered, that put me in such a helpless, naive state? I was usually so organised, and yet here I relied on people like Anastasia to put me on track: the Helena of my return, another beneficent spirit ensuring I made it to the Pirate's taverna. The ancients would have called it fate.

It worked. Two hours later I was on a bus to Karousades. By half-ten, I was climbing into the hills of the north. There, the brightness of morning was dulled by a growing heat haze; a full bus at the start gradually emptied as we paused at the small stops on the way. Passengers disembarked into narrow streets and near taverna car parks.

I had asked to be told when we were close to Karousades. 'Sit!' the conductor said when he saw me straining to see where we were. 'I will tell you,' he barked, the intention friendly.

After an hour, I got a nod from his rear-view mirror to indicate that we were reaching Karousades. I didn't recognise the stop. I was thrown by a change to the bus route, which didn't go all the way into the village anymore, to the Pirate's front bench. Instead, we stopped at the base of the hill road into the village.

I stepped off and collected my bag from the hold, and for a moment stood beside a café, trying to figure out where I was exactly. Along the café's front porch, a group of men sat sipping coffee and smoking, as though they'd been waiting all morning for this precise moment when a straggler would show up. 'Kalimera,' I said.

They waved in unison. I sat down, ordered a coffee and took out the Pirate's business card. I turned to the men. 'Could I ask you a question? I'm looking for someone who used to live here.'

Two stood and came over. 'Who do you want?' said one.

'There was a taverna in the village.' I handed them the business card. 'I think the owner's name was Elisseos.'

'Yes.'

'Do you know him?' I asked.

'Of course,' he answered matter-of-factly. 'He lives up there. He has the taverna.' He pointed up the hill towards the village.

'Really?'

The man seemed confused by *my* confusion. Then again, he didn't know that twenty-four years had passed since I was last here. But how could everything be exactly as it was? 'It is closed now,' the man continued. 'Go later. Tonight. Not now. It will be open for dinner.'

'Okay, I'll wait until tonight,' I said, and sipped my coffee in disbelief.

'Where are you staying?' the man asked.

I took out my accommodation voucher and confessed that I didn't know how to get there from here. I showed them the address. There was a round of consultations and calling out to the others in the taverna. They made a scooter rider stop and read the voucher. He said the apartment I'd booked was at the end of a narrow lane that wound through olive groves and fenced gardens of goats and vegetables down to the beach.

'Really?' I said again. That's where the Pirate's villa had been.

'Yes,' said the scooter rider, I think a little affronted by my astonishment, and rode off.

I fancied I could hear their thoughts. Who *was* this strange man the morning bus had brought in, who seemed unable to accept perfectly commonplace facts about the village and the beach? But perhaps I had started to see the story as a fiction, just like my friends in Brisbane who'd been made to hear it and expressed their doubts. Improbable, at least.

As I walked down the hill to my apartment, I reminded myself that there was no rule saying things *had* to change. But my life was so different now; it was strange to find that the island I'd left behind had stayed the way it was.

The road down to the sea was almost as spooky as before, but not quite. There were no shepherdesses calling out from wooden huts. But I did hear dogs barking as I walked past farms, and I felt the solitude of the path as I had before; these things put me on edge, directed my thoughts towards unlikely scenarios. What if Olanda was right and the Pirate came at me with a cleaver, enraged by the years he'd spent waiting for his eighty dollars?

You never posted the money, you bastard!

I trusted you. I even said I loved you!

I let you go. My friends. I let you go.

My imagination settled down when I got to my apartment and unpacked my things, gave myself a sense of settling in. The balcony looked across a bay paled by the noon sun, and towards the hills across the channel. I recalled that the villagers had feared the Albanian cannons on the other side, which they claimed were directed at Corfu. The idea seemed oddly historical, like a cover of a matchbox packet in a social history museum – made quaint by the passage of time, much like my own fears. I was being ridiculous: the Pirate wouldn't care about a debt that was this old.

It would be late in Brisbane by now, but I video-called Olanda and the boys. They answered from the study, the picture grainy to begin with, then over-exposed by a lamp on the desk. The boys wanted to be centre frame and crowded in front of Olanda, their heads close together and bumping. It was only a week since I'd left for the conference, but seeing them and remembering their constant movement, their ceaseless energy, made it feel like longer. My heart ached with a wish to be with them in person.

'Did you find him?' asked Finnur.

'Sort of. I found out the taverna is still there and he still runs it. Can you believe it? I'm going to go up and see it tonight!'

'Oh no,' said Olanda.

'Yes!' said Finnur. 'You found the Pirate!'

Magnús pushed his head in front of Finnur. 'Mum thinks he's going to kill you,' he said.

'That's not what I said at all!' Olanda protested, laughing. 'I said I was *nervous* about Dad seeing him.' Before I left Brisbane, she extracted a promise from me that I'd be careful and not put myself in harm's way. But by now, I thought, surely any possible malice in the Pirate was like his nickname: a trope. He must be old, piracy over and done with. I hoped so.

'Do you think he'll come after you?' asked Finnur. It was all a bit of a joke, but there was a touch of nervousness there, too. He was looking after me from the other side of the world.

'Well, he *is* a pirate,' I said, teasingly, not wanting to worry him. 'They're not known for their good manners. But it's a very long time ago. No-one can be annoyed for *that* long.'

'No-one?' asked Olanda. 'Aren't you still annoyed with yourself for doing the runner?'

'Yes, something like that,' I said.

We hung up, and suddenly I felt less sure about everything. What the hell was I doing? I asked myself. Who travelled all the way to Greece to pay an eighty-dollar debt from 1990? I truly *was* like my young self again, unknowing, standing at the edge of a ferry dock. There might have been something sweet about that in an eighteen-year-old. But in a father of two in his forties?

It was time to shake myself out of it. I looked outside. It was early afternoon, and warm. I unpacked and changed into shorts and a T-shirt and walked down the lane next to my apartment for a swim. The water was shallow, the shoreline coated with brown seagrass. I was the only one there. I floated on the surface, listening to the scratch of the waves against the pebble shore. It was blissful and I could quite easily have spent the whole day there.

As always after a swim, my mood lifted, and I began to look forward to going back up the hill. I came in off the beach and showered, and waited impatiently until five, when I thought the Pirate's taverna might open, or he might be prepping for the night. At five-thirty, I retraced my steps past the new bus stop into the village.

The streets were still empty; the taverna wasn't open yet, either. I peered inside. Much of it was entirely the same, down to the arrangement of the small tables, the bottles on the wall, a television in the corner. The only difference I could see was that the old wooden kitchen bench had been replaced with a steel one. Could time really have made such an indiscernible impression?

Evidently. For the village, too, was unchanged, only a bit older and more tired, still in need of whitewashing, but otherwise spared from tourism by its distance from the sea and its roads being too narrow for the larger buses that now crisscrossed the island. At this hour of the day, I couldn't find anywhere to sit and wait for the Pirate's taverna to open, until I chanced upon an open door: a tiny bar and, inside, the owner washing down a grill.

'Hello?' I said. 'Could I get a beer?'

'Yes, sit down. Outside in the sun, if you like. Please, take a seat.'

The barman said he needed to keep cleaning but eventually he came out to talk. His name was Alexandre and he'd been living in Karousades for a year – his wife was from the village; he was an Athenian. They'd arrived from the capital with their newborn child; I could hear it making contented sounds that wafted down from the upstairs window.

'I'm as happy as I can ever remember,' Alexandre said.

I could well imagine it. In my mind's eye, I could still see the boys jostling for space on the screen, and I wished they were with me now, watching the village reawaken after the lull of the afternoon.

I told Alexandre that I was here to visit the Pirate. 'His name is Elisseos. I've heard he still has his taverna.'

'Yes, he's still here,' said Alexandre, smiling. 'He will open later. Sit. Take your time.' He went back inside and resumed his cleaning and setting up.

A single scooter went past, but no other traffic. After an hour, there were the sounds of footsteps and people talking, shop doors being unlocked, the green light of the pharmacy flickering on, and the village finally came to life.

I was getting more nervous. I closed my eyes and listened to the village, to shift my thoughts to the world around me. An evening breeze in the trees. Alexandre's baby laughing. More scooters. Sweeping on porches, as always. A voice, an evening greeting across the street. Drink crates being dragged to a taverna back door. My fingers tapping the table.

Time passing. Minutes. Years, as well.

The year appearing again as what it really was, what it became for the boys when I told it to them. A year of adventures and risks, troubles, and solutions, experiences I hoped they would have as well one day. That I would have to *let* my children have, if I wasn't going to stand in their way.

Given how little else had changed in Karousades, maybe I shouldn't have been surprised that the Pirate would be sitting exactly as I had found him in the evenings back in 1990. Corner table, sipping coffee, waiting for customers to come in so he could get up and stir life into the tables, shake the depths and distances out of his reflections. A taverna like this was always a place where someone stands at the door and hopes to be waved in. Waits for the signal. He obliged: 'Come in!' he called to me. 'Welcome!'

He hadn't changed at all. Well, I say that, but his hair was no longer black, and instead a dull grey, though it was still long. The slow menace and anger that had once filled his eyes had become something more like heaviness. His clothes were rather worse, too, but still involved a light-blue T-shirt besmeared with cooking oil and wine. It was as surely the Pirate as it was the taverna, the village, the island.

As I thought might be the case when he saw me, he had no idea who I was. 'Hello,' I said. 'Can I have dinner here tonight?'

'Yes. Half an hour. Sit down. Have wine first. The grill isn't hot.'

He showed me to a table near the front windows and joined me. The television was playing news of Greece's debt negotiations. A time for debts the world over, I thought; people being interviewed complained the country would never be able to pay the foreign banks. The kitchen was busy with preparations for the night's trade, but the Pirate wasn't taking any part. It was all being done by a man and his son, a boy of around twelve or thirteen who was doing most of the running around, fetching ingredients, clearing tables.

'I knew you when I was young,' I said after a moment watching them work. 'I've come back to see you.'

'Hmm?'

'Twenty-five years ago.'

The Pirate studied me a little more carefully. He didn't see it. 'You know me?'

'I worked here on the island when I was eighteen. You helped me to find work. You were very good to me.'

The Pirate squinted and shook his head. Perhaps it was the language difference, which seemed more acute now, or I'd brought it up too quickly, but he wasn't convinced he knew me. So many visitors to the island must have passed through his life since I'd been here. 'What is your name?' he asked.

I told him, but he remained just as unsure. 'I had long hair,' I said. 'I was very thin, as well.'

'Oh,' he said. I got the feeling he wasn't enjoying this test of his memory.

'How is your mother?' I asked, changing tact. 'I knew her, too.'

He shook his head. 'She died,' he said. 'Two years ago.'

'I'm sorry. I'm sorry I missed seeing her.'

Still, he couldn't recollect me. I took out his business card, the one I'd found in my old leather bag. His eyebrows rose at this, and he seemed to search more pressingly for me among the drifters who'd turned up here over the years. He flipped the card over and read printed text that was on the front.

'Chrisos!' he said.

'Really, Chrisos? Is that his address?'

'Yes.'

It was my memory's turn to falter. How had Chrisos's business card come to be used when the Pirate wrote down his details? Surely he wasn't there when we'd made our escape? 'Does Chrisos still live in the village?' I asked.

'Dead,' said the Pirate. 'Hit on his scooter.'

'Oh, no,' I said.

'Yes. He rode very badly,' said the Pirate. 'Dangerous. Too fast.'

I mentioned that Chrisos used to give us rides to the campground and to the beach. I remembered how wildly he would ride down the hill. 'There were three of us who worked together,' I went on. 'Me and Felix and Paul. Do you remember them?'

'Felix, yes, him.' But that recollection didn't lead to one of me. 'Felix has visited,' the Pirate said. 'He is okay.' So it wasn't just me: Felix had wanted to come back, too. His own debts to pay, no doubt.

'I have a photo,' I said.

I showed him the photo I'd printed out in Brisbane, of Paul, Felix and me with the Pirate and the Swedish couple. He peered at it and smiled. Yes, there *was* a version of me that he could remember in there, someone he'd known in those days. But was it really me, the one here in the taverna with him now?

He scrutinised me again and laughed. 'The years go like that!' he exclaimed. 'Pssfp! Fucking hell!'

'How old are you now?' I asked.

'I am fifty-nine,' he said. 'How old are you?'

I was about to turn forty-two. It didn't seem so much of an age difference now, only seventeen years. In 1990, it had been the entirety of my life.

We kept talking. I still didn't think he fully remembered me, even though he seemed to accept the evidence and recognise the young man in the photo. When I told him that Paul and I had stayed in his villa, he boasted that it had a second level now, and his farm had a proper house on it. And, yes, the wooden bench in front of the taverna had been replaced. The shoe shop was closed, the shoe sellers gone. He gave me these updates as you would to a person whom you knew, and yet, when he looked at me, I could tell there was a blank that would take much longer than one dinner service to fill.

'Changes,' I said. 'I was thinking how everything's stayed the same here, but time passes. We only called you Pirate. I don't think I ever used your name. Why were you called the Pirate?'

'I am a sailor. You're from Australia. I went to Melbourne many times. Are you from Melbourne?'

'No.'

'All the Greeks! You walk down the street and then, "Hey you *malakas!*" Fucking hell.'

He was ready to go, begin the Pirate act, one that I knew well enough. I didn't want to hear it, not just then. What I hoped for right now was some way of conveying to him the reason I was here. How could I say thank you if he didn't even understand what I was thanking him for?

'You were very good to us,' I said, attempting to redirect the conversation. 'We owed you money and you let us go without paying.'

The Pirate didn't understand. He didn't remember the moment at all. 'Drink,' he said instead. 'It is good wine. My wine!'

I took a sip. Nothing much was happening in the kitchen or on the grill yet. Dinner must be hours off, I thought. There was a moment of silence, and I wasn't sure what to say. 'Actually,' I stumbled, 'I need to pop out to buy some coffee to have at my apartment.'

The Pirate shook his head and called over the cook's son, the boy who'd been setting up. Already, he'd come over twice to tell the Pirate that something was missing in the kitchen, and rather slowly the Pirate had extracted crumpled euro notes from his pocket so that the boy could buy the missing ingredients. Now, he told the boy to take me to get coffee.

As we ambled down the street to the corner shop, the boy called out to everyone and seemed to know all the goings-on.

'Where are you from?' I asked.

'Albania,' he said. 'I live here with my father. We like it.'

'I can see that,' I said. 'It looks like you know everyone.'

'My mother will come to Corfu one day, as well.'

When we got back, I had the impression that he adored the Pirate, too. There was a touch of Felix in him and in how familiar he was with the Pirate, although he was younger and gentler in nature than Felix had been. But the Pirate's parental bearing towards him was as strong.

As the shadows lengthened, the Pirate became more alert, and some faint memories of me seemed to leak back. He asked me about Felix and Paul again, and gradually I think he located our shared place in his past. As others walked in for dinner, the first customers of the night, he asked me what I was doing these days.

'I teach at a university,' I said. 'I write. Travel stories, books.'

He nodded. 'Are you going to write about me?'

'I'd like to, yes.'

'What will you say?'

'I want to write a story about someone who helped me when I was young.' And, I hoped, a second part, too: about this moment now, when, in later life, we return to the past and tell it to those we love, a sharing and letting in that is part of being a parent.

The Pirate eyed me closely and said, 'I hope you get it right.'

At eight-thirty, my dinner was served. The Pirate didn't eat, but he wouldn't leave my side while I worked my way through a banquet of grilled chicken, salad, peppers, chips and bread. The food was as good as I remembered it.

It was getting dark outside, and the street was busy with pedestrians now. Some waved and yell-talked to the Pirate when they saw him. I wasn't looking forward to the walk down the hill to my apartment. 'I'm going to go soon,' I said to the Pirate, 'before it's completely dark.'

'One more glass of wine,' he said. 'Then you can go.'

I took the glass. 'What kind of wine is this?'

'My wine,' he said. 'From my farm.'

'Yes, I know, but what kind of grape. What variety is it?'

I didn't understand what he said in reply; it was a Greek word. I asked him to write it down in my notebook: *Szafili*, he wrote.

I said I'd look it up and, with that, the Pirate and I toasted one last time. 'Thank you, Pirate,' I said.

I waited until he was called to the kitchen before I left. Then, I took out the printed photograph of us, folded it over, and inside it I placed twenty euros for dinner and sixty euros for the debt – the dinners and wines and rent and cigarettes of twenty-five years before. It wasn't really enough for all he'd done, and probably I should have added some late fees, but it was something, at least.

I stood up. 'Goodbye, Pirate,' I called.

'Are you going so early?' he asked, seeming to have forgotten what I'd just said. He stepped across the dining room and held my shoulder while he shook my hand with his free one. 'Come again,' he said. 'You are welcome here.'

I knew already that I wouldn't come back, not on that trip, at least. I wasn't embarrassed by him not knowing who I was, or disappointed about it. In fact, I felt overwhelmed with joy that I was here, and that I'd had a chance to return some of what I owed him. The satisfaction in that act of payment was very deep, and much more rewarding than the matter of whether he remembered me. It was all I wanted, for now. For me to go back for another dinner with him would have prolonged something that felt perfect.

There was still a touch of light in the sky as I walked back to the apartment, and the road to the beach was not as bad, just as the Pirate was not as bad either. Not these days. It wasn't very often that you got to return like this: to a past world to find it so well preserved. Maybe, if I'd stayed, I would be sitting at the taverna with him, unchanged as well. Eighteen forever, like a character in a fairy tale.

Was the Pirate a pirate?

Yes, of course he was.

Brazil, Brazil! Who else but a pirate would carry on like that? But he was also *this* Pirate, an open and hospitable man who made friends with boys who ran out of money, who grew his own olives and grapes, and sang along to ballads of heartbreak and longing. A tired old drunk who didn't want his guests to leave. So many nights, countless nights, until they couldn't be held apart. A survivor of his own drifting.

Szafili, he'd written in my journal. I googled it that night; it didn't appear to be a variety at all. It seems *Szafili*, or *stafili* as it is also spelt, is simply the Greek word for *grape*. It was a broad term, like *pirate*.

The following morning, I called home and told Olanda and the boys that he'd been there, and that I'd paid him, and that I was still alive. I sent them a photo, too, that the Pirate had insisted on having taken – of the two of us raising a glass of his wine.

'Did he remember you?' Finnur asked.

'Not really. Well, not at first. We sort of got there in the end.'

'So he wouldn't have remembered the debt, either,' Olanda said.

'No, not a bit of it. I guess I wasn't the first or last person who didn't pay him the bill.'

'But you were his boys!' said Magnús.

'I know. He actually remembers Felix pretty well. But not me or Paul. It was only when I showed him the picture that he started to.'

'But you've done it, anyway,' Finnur said, as though I needed to be reassured the trip was worthwhile. 'You paid him.'

'You paid him, Dad,' reiterated Magnús.

When we hung up, I thought about it again. Should I be upset that he didn't know me, I wondered? Was the imbalance an important one? I took those questions with me as I went for a morning walk, planning to seek out the Pirate's villa, now finished. No. It didn't matter, I was sure of it. The gift he'd given me in those years before was what mattered then, and what mattered just as much now. And that was because it wasn't a debt that I carried on my own. It was a family story, a debt to be paid together.

17

The true debt

Corfu, September 2022

At the beginning of this book, I wrote that I wanted to tell a story about looking for one's younger self. That this can be worth doing, even necessary, because there are aspects of who we were that get left behind, but can be reclaimed if we want to. When we need that person back for a moment. I said our younger self might even help us with something in the present, if we listen well enough, and attend to how they were, and what they were capable of.

So, what did I find?

To start with, many things that I wouldn't do now, but perhaps need to re-learn how to do, so that I am at least capable of seeing my sons enjoy the kinds of adventures that I did. A deeper trust in the world, despite its fullness of vices. A willingness to go along with the road, to be directed by chance. An ability to accept that loss is part of change, but that we recover, just as I did from the loss of my father.

There. All fixed? Not quite. I'll admit I'm finding it hard. The sense of loss I feel now that the boys are getting older is not a mirage or a misperception. It's real because the changes are real. Every day, I notice how much they've matured, and I pine for the little boys they once were – how the space between us was almost non-existent. Now that they're reaching the age I was when I first arrived in Corfu, they are also reaching the start of their own adventures and misadventures. The space between us expands. What if they're dragged into piracy of some kind? Will they be let go, like I was?

But the true debt that I owe to the Pirate is located in the person I truly was; that is, beyond the hapless free spirit who washed up onto his shores. Beyond my recklessness and naivety. I think he let me go so that I could be that person. I was no pirate, no buccaneer. I was a son who wanted to become a father, and run with my own pirates, instead. The real Pirate saw that, and had no wish to hold me back from what surely struck him as the most terrible fate of all, which of course is a settled family life.

It's our fourth day in Corfu since Olanda and the boys joined me. Tomorrow, we're shifting to Kalami Bay for a week, where things will be more like a holiday; we can sit on the beach and do day trips and walk to dinner in the evening. I think of Michelle and how she recommended it to me after she'd gone there to trace the steps of the Durrells.

When we started organising this trip a few months ago, I hadn't been able to find out much more about the Pirate than I could before I returned to Corfu in 2014. He wasn't online, but that didn't mean that he wasn't still welcoming guests to his taverna, and I imagined the four of us turning up and being shown to a table, and Olanda and the boys meeting the Pirate for themselves, which they wanted to do. But we also knew things might have changed in the eight years since I last visited.

I broke my journey from Brisbane to Karousades with two nights in Corfu Town. It was late August and very hot, but jet lag had me waking up at four in the morning; I used the cooler sunrise hours to go for a walk around the town. It can be disorienting to be on a different body clock from both those at home and the people around you, but you get to meet the somewhat hidden world of those whose daily work takes place in that in-between time, and in a city's preparations for the day ahead. The smooth cobble lanes were being hosed clean, becoming glossy brown; delivery trucks reversed into impossibly narrow bays; and the docks were being readied for the first ferries, each ship with its own promises of arrival, and the joy of experiencing Corfu for the first time.

It was there – at the ferry terminal, at dawn – that I felt the sensation of time travel most acutely, of going back to the moment Paul and I arrived in 1990. But I knew I was going to be joined by my family in a few weeks, a prospect that robbed the moment of its nostalgia. Happily so. I didn't want to convince my sons of a 'better' past. How could I, when I had so much to be pleased with now? When I had them? If our task was to share the events of my youth, then it was for the sake of our time together now. To bring the past along with us, if possible.

I'm convinced we've managed to do that over the past few days together. The journey has been a dual one: both my story and the boys' impressions and thoughts. It has helped me understand my sense of loss but also to see the promise of their futures coming into view. Fatherhood ultimately faces forwards rather than back.

They will not get to meet the Pirate. The closest thing they will get to that is my memories of him, the village, and the picture on the bench in his taverna, the one I showed them on their first day.

Now, on our final evening before we leave Karousades, we decide to take a last, long walk through the village. Olanda and the boys say that they could spend longer here: they don't mind its separateness, the feeling of being a little cut off. It's still possible to buy a house or apartment fairly cheaply here. As we walk down the hill towards the square, we fantasise about what it would be like having a place in Greece to come to every year. 'We'd better finish paying the school fees first,' I say. 'You two cost us a fortune,' as I remind them every week or so.

Sometimes, when I tell friends that I once made a trip to Greece to pay a pirate eighty dollars that I'd owed him from twenty-five years before, they joke that I probably owe a fair bit of interest as well. So I've checked. At an annual interest rate of fifteen per cent with a loan term of twenty-five years, my repayments would be two dollars per month with total interest payable of about two hundred and thirty dollars. That's to say, even after I paid the eighty dollars, I still owed the Pirate a bit of money. I don't mind that, to be honest.

The boys go ahead while Olanda and I lock up the apartment. I'm not sure we really need to, and in any case the French windows that open onto the balcony don't lock properly. Over the weeks that I've been here, the villagers seem to have gotten used to the sight of me heading out for my afternoon walks or, before I got the scratched hatchback, waiting at the bus stop for buses that sometimes come. I've started getting waves and hellos, as we do now, while we stroll down the hill to the first of the village squares.

*

The Pirate drew his last breath a few months ago, in the winter just gone. I found out the sad news on my first day in the village. After I'd caught the bus from Corfu Town and dropped my bags at my apartment, I went straight to the taverna. I found the photo of him on the dividing bench, beside a vase of flowers.

I wasn't surprised to discover that the Pirate had passed away. In many ways, it was more surprising that he'd lived as long as he did. But I felt the shock of it, all the same. Over the decades, I'd carried his presence with me as more than a person to whom I owed money, whom I had wronged in some way. I cared about him – even if he couldn't remember me very well when we met again, and probably wouldn't have had a clue who I was now.

I was about to go back to the apartment when I heard some banging in the property next door, another former taverna. It no longer appeared to serve customers, its chairs piled against a back wall. Two women were preparing pizza bases: flattening the dough, wrapping it and building a pile. I knocked on the door and said hello.

'Do you need something?' one asked. 'We're not open, sorry.'

I said I'd come to see Elisseos, and that I'd just seen the photo.

'Yes, Elisseos died,' she said. 'Did you know him?'

'I did,' I said. 'Years ago. I'm sorry that he's passed away.'

The woman put aside her work for a moment and we talked about what had happened. I had the feeling it wasn't the first time she'd been asked. She said the Pirate was sick for some months before he died and had been in hospital. But, also, that he was very much at peace with his time coming to an end. She added he'd lived a rich life and knew that this had its costs; he didn't resent the choices he'd made. We all had to go eventually, after all.

I could see they had a lot of work to do. The other woman

in the kitchen hadn't stopped bringing things out as part of their preparations. 'They're not for the village,' she said. 'We sell all our food to the tavernas down at the beach.'

'You look busy,' I said. I thanked the first woman for letting me know about the Pirate, and was about to leave, but she had a little more to say.

'Elisseos was a very special person in the village,' she began. 'We loved him. Thousands of people knew him, from all around the world. They came just to see him, just like you. We will miss him very much.'

'I met his mother as well,' I said. 'She used to work in the kitchen.'

'Oh, you met her too! Yes, she was an incredible woman. She made sure he behaved himself.' She smiled at the thought. 'We Greek women are like that.'

I walked back to the apartment and texted Olanda and the boys to let them know the Pirate had died. It was evening in Brisbane, and they wrote back, sad about the news and hoping I was okay. *Yes, I'm fine*, I wrote back, although I was more upset than I wanted to admit. *He was quite old. Apparently, he was ready for it when it came.* That wasn't really the point, I knew: grief is not hostage to logical calculations of when someone is likely to have died. It somehow seemed more like I was losing a relative or a family friend, and I was sending messages to an extended family he didn't know. I wrote to Mum as well.

Left with my own thoughts, I sat on the balcony and tried to understand a depth of sadness that was rather unexpected. I felt for him as a person who was probably rather alone, even if the village and thousands of visitors cared deeply for him and kept him company. Perhaps, too, there was a link to other losses in my life, especially my own father's passing and having not known him very well when he was alive. But most of all, I was sad because I had lost a friend, however unusual a friendship it might have been.

The next day, I set up a writing table near the balcony windows and tried to settle down to work. At first, I couldn't concentrate. I was still jetlagged and disoriented by the fact that it was only the second day of a three-week stay in the village, and there wasn't really anything more to *do*. The Pirate was gone. What was left, then?

The following day, I began my routine of walking and swimming at Astrakeri beach, chatting to the half-English barman. On my way back to the apartment, I bought meat from the village butcher. He complained about business, said everything was on the decline in the village. He was about my age. The shop had been his father's, he told me. He brought out a large side of beef and cut off a steak on a round wooden block that stood in the middle of the shop. 'This is how we do it here,' he said. 'I never keep anything in the cabinet. That's what supermarkets do, not butchers.'

Later that day, I introduced myself to my neighbours, a couple in their seventies who lived in one of the townhouses in my street. Georgios and Andromeda invited me in and asked me to sit down in their living room. Andromeda said she couldn't speak English and left for the kitchen, and then came back with slices of watermelon, which she placed on the coffee table in front of me. Georgios, meanwhile, launched into a bit of a questionnaire, one that seemed made for new arrivals like me: age, occupation, family status, income, property holdings.

I answered his questions happily, as I had some of my own.

I was hoping to discover a little more about Elisseos's last years. Georgios, as one might have guessed from his questions to me, was across all the details. We settled in for a chat.

He said it was a heart condition that got the better of Elisseos in the end. Georgios tapped his chest. He said Elisseos had never married and there were no children. After his death, it was discovered – to everyone's great surprise – that the Pirate had been a great money saver: he'd amassed real wealth, diligently putting all his earnings straight in the bank. Because he was childless, it all went to his sister. Georgios's eyes widened.

'I didn't know he had a sister,' I said.

'Yes, careful with his money,' he said, approvingly. 'A clever man.'

Clever. Money-wise. A special person in the village, much loved and missed. A magnet for visitors. If pirates were meant to be selfish and reckless, thieves and spoilers who placed individual greed and adventure ahead of the communities they raided, then it appeared that, by the time he died, the Pirate was not anything like a pirate anymore. He was an old man in an old village, loved, and grieved by all now that he was gone.

Including me. Looking back, I think the Pirate was most probably a shy, perhaps even solitary, man concealed under an act that allowed him to appear very social and involved and gave him the basis of friendship with those who drifted into the village. Often, the most hospitable people we know spend a lot of time getting things ready for others. They opt for the tasks of service.

*

As this will be our last look at the village, we take a more roundabout route, beginning with a side street that veers towards a football field and the road to the next village. It's true that many of the old homes are dilapidated, some even derelict. But here and there, renovations are underway: new roofs being put on, kitchens and air conditioners sitting on the pavement waiting to be installed. I hope they're not all being done up for tourist apartments like ours. The lessons of the past are not always easy to quantify, and probably shouldn't be read too literally. But the prosperity in Karousades's proud history may offer guideposts.

The boys have been walking a hundred metres ahead of me and Olanda. When we reach them, they're watching a football team training on the local club's field. We stand with them for a while until Finnur asks, 'Are you glad you came back?'

'I'm glad you've had a chance to see the village. Even though the Pirate's not alive, I do feel like I've introduced you to him. Having you here changes how I see him and what happened.'

'Hmm?'

'I'm very grateful that I got to come here when I did, that Paul and I found ourselves in Corfu, but I'm also very grateful that we got away.'

'But you could have gone to Brazil. That would be cool.'

'Just promise me you'll never agree to a deal like that,' I say. 'The rest I can handle, I think.'

'Alright, I promise. No pirate runs to South America for me.'

I resist the temptation to add more prohibitions as we loop back around the village to the front of the taverna again. 'Well?' I say, as the boys and I pose for a photo. 'Thoughts?'

Magnús jumps in. 'You did the right thing getting away when you did.'

217

'Definitely,' says Finnur, modifying his earlier position.

'Maybe I'd still be in there today, if I hadn't,' I suggest. 'Sitting at a corner table, getting drunk every night, singing ballads about my broken heart.' I put my arms around the boys and pull them close for a kiss. 'I love you, boys,' I say.

They say they love me, too, and wipe the wet off their cheeks.

We begin walking back towards where the car is parked. By the time we get there, the boys have marched on ahead again, stretching their legs against the rise in the road as they go. They wait for us next to the back doors. I can guess what they're talking about: whose turn it is to sit behind me, as my seat is always back further. As we jump in, I search for something to say to mark the moment: the change in our travels now that we're leaving the village. My passage from loss to a growing sense of acceptance.

I start the car and open the windows instead, and feel the warm air blowing over me, like the vents at the rear of the ferry. Our carton of cigarettes was gone, stolen, or maybe they'd just slid across the ferry floor and into the sea.

That morning when I stood up and gazed across the channel, at dawn, and waited for Paul to find me: I didn't know what was going to happen next, but when we looked at each other I was sure that the silence had solved it. I'd been waiting for a place like this, just like now, where we could figure it out, our own questions. There was no going back, but that didn't matter anymore because suddenly the feeling was of arrival, anticipation. A fire island coming into view, burning with the first direct light, its pale buildings altered into a beacon that was the length of the coast. An insistence to disembark and see it closer, smell its streets and tavernas and gardens, feel the morning chill disappear and the arrival of the heat of a late-summer afternoon, the touch of water so clear that I could see the sand and dark boulders at the bottom.

At the Pirate's taverna, Karousades, Corfu, 14 September 2022

Acknowledgements

As this is a book about family, friendship and place, it couldn't be written without the generosity and goodwill of the many people featured in its two stories. I would especially like to thank my wife, Olanda, and our two sons, Finnur Kári and Magnús Oliver, for being such warm-hearted collaborators and for joining me in Corfu in September 2022. To my mother, Susan, I am indebted for her open and gracious conversations about the past. I also remain very grateful to the Pirate, to Paul, and to the people I met and grew to love when I first travelled to the village of Karousades, a place that affected me deeply then, as it has on subsequent returns.

This book was written in part in Karousades; I thank my hosts for the rental of their apartment in the village. It was completed in Brisbane, or Meanjin, on the lands of the Turrbal and Yugara peoples, whom I also respectfully acknowledge as the traditional owners of where I live and work. Throughout, I have been supported by friends and colleagues at the School of Creative Practice, Queensland University of Technology, and buoyed by the enthusiasm and talent of my students.

My gratitude also goes to those who've helped me to develop this work through conversations and in feedback they've given on the manuscript while it was in draft form: my agent at Left Bank Literary, Grace Heifetz, as well as Richard Fidler, Mauro Liberatore, Courtney Pedersen, Fiona Reilly and Emma Sartori. Sincere thanks to Nick Earls and Susan Johnson for offering very kind cover endorsements, to Lisa White for her evocative cover design, and to Nicholas Martin for taking author photos.

Finally, I would like to express my deep appreciation to everyone at UQP: in particular, Sarah Valle and the marketing and publicity team, and my publisher Madonna Duffy and editor Ian See, who did so much to help me to understand the story that I was telling in these pages, and to improve its balance of elements.

Σας ευχαριστώ!

Also by Kári Gíslason

THE PROMISE OF ICELAND

In 1990, at the age of seventeen, Kári Gíslason travelled to Iceland, the land of his birth, and arranged to meet his father. What he found was not what he expected.

Born from a secret liaison between his British mother and Icelandic father, Kári moved regularly between Iceland, England and Australia. He grew up aware of who his father was, but understood his mother had promised never to reveal his father's identity. It was a promise his father would also ask him to keep.

A decade later, Kári made the decision to break that promise, and he contacted his half-siblings, who knew nothing of his existence. What led him to this decision and what followed makes for a heartfelt and riveting journey traversing landscapes, time and memory, of one man's search for a sense of belonging.

> 'A deeply charming account of displacement, of not really knowing where you come from and how that makes it difficult to know where you belong.' *The Sunday Mail*

978 0 7022 3906 9

THE SORROW STONE

After committing an audacious act of revenge for her brother's murder, Disa flees with her son through the fjords of Iceland. She has already endured the death of her loved ones. Now she must run to save her son, and her honour.

In a society where betrayals and revenge killings are rife, all Disa has is her pride and her courage. Will it be enough for her and her son to escape retribution?

Dramatic and urgent in its telling, *The Sorrow Stone* celebrates one woman's quest, against the dramatic backdrop of the Icelandic countryside. In this gripping novel, the co-author of the bestselling *Saga Land* takes a sidelined figure from the Viking tales and finally puts her where she belongs – at the centre of the story.

'A masterly retelling of one of Iceland's most famous sagas ... I found it utterly captivating.' Hannah Kent

'This epic tale transported me to another time and place completely.' Favel Parrett

978 0 7022 6552 5